A Madrasi Memoir

Renuka Narayanan is a commentator and columnist on religion and culture. She was Arts Editor, *The Indian Express* with a column on religion; Editor, Religion & Culture, *Hindustan Times*; and the start-up Director of the Indian Cultural Centre, Embassy of India, Bangkok. Her published books include *The Book of Prayer, Faith: Filling the God-sized Hole* and *The Little Book of Indian Wisdom*.

A Madrasi Memoir

RENUKA NARAYANAN

E
LIMITED
EDITIONS

First published in 2016
by
LIMITED EDITIONS
an imprint of

ACADEMIC FOUNDATION

Delhi Sales Office:
4772-73 / 23 Bharat Ram Road,
(23 Ansari Road), Darya Ganj,
New Delhi - 110 002 (India).
Phones : 23245001 / 02 / 03 / 04.
Fax : +91-11-23245005.

Corporate Office:
No. 35, Sector 7,
IMT Manesar,
Gurgaon - 122050.
Haryana (India).
Tel: +91-124-4215070 / 71.

E-mail : books@academicfoundation.com
www.academicfoundation.org

Disclaimer:
The findings/views/opinions expressed in this book are solely those of the author and do not necessarily reflect the views of the publisher.

Inside photographs: courtesy, author.

Cataloging in Publication Data--DK
Courtesy: D.K. Agencies (P) Ltd. <docinfo@dkagencies.com>

Renuka Narayanan, author.
A Madrasi Memoir / Renuka Narayanan.
pages cm
ISBN 9789332703704

1. Renuka Narayanan. 2. Tamil (Indic people)--India--Chennai--Biography. 3. Brahmans--India--Chennai--Biography. I. Title.

DS432.B73K43 2016 DDC 305.6945092 23

Printed and bound by The Book Mint, New Delhi.
www.thebookmint.in

For Anya and Advait

But have you wine and music still,
And statues and a bright-eyed love,
And foolish thoughts of good and ill,
And prayers to them who sit above?
- James Elroy Flecker

- *One* -

My first memory of life is of a stinging slap on my cheek. I was four years old and lived on Poorna Das Road, Calcutta. I was then the only child of my parents, a brahmin couple from Madras in their early thirties. I was slapped by my father's elder sister, Kanti Sastri, who was on a visit from Delhi where she taught at university.

It seems I went still with shock at the new experience and turned questioning eyes at my mother, Kausalya, who looked back at me without saying a word. My father, six feet tall, with long bones and a long face like the central figure in Amrita Shergil's painting *Brahmins* but minus the forehead-mark, was silent, too.

"Never say that again," said my aunt into the silence. It seems I nodded and trained already in appropriate responses by my mother, said, "Sorry." My parents left without another word for their jobs as revenue officers and Mahua Sinha, my day-minder, an educated married

In Calcutta, soon to be slapped.

lady who was permitted by her family to take up this work, took me out of the room. Our cook, a middle-aged brahmin man from Madras, was put on the train south next day though naturally I do not remember that part.

The cook had referred to our sweeper-lady as a *parachi*, an 'outcaste' or 'untouchable' woman. I had repeated the word without knowing the meaning and was promptly slapped hard by my aunt. My parents wholly endorsed her action by their silence and my mother fired and despatched the cook as a corrupting influence in her household.

That night I was taken by my aunt and mother to the grassy open ground outside our block of government flats. The sky was full of stars.

"Look," said my aunt, pointing to the sky. "Valentina Tereshkova is up there in her spaceship".

"She's a Russian scientist," said my mother. "Spell 'Russia'".

"Spell 'Valentina Tereshkova' if you want a *sondesh* from Ganguram's," said my father who had strolled out to join us.

These are my two earliest memories, from a day in June 1963, and there is a third from that time, of the first song I learned, which was the first verse of the Tamil 'Shaiva bible', the *Thirumurai*. It was the first song ever learned by my father, also at age four, as a child in Madras, and by his father before him and so on, back into previous generations.

My father had a fine singing voice resembling Talat Mehmood's and the song he taught me, *Thodudaya cheviyan*, about Shiva, was composed by Sambandar, a young poet-saint in the seventh century CE. Sambandar was one of the sixty-three Nayanmar, the Shaiva poet-saints who lived in the Tamil region between the sixth and the tenth centuries. As I write this, less than four years short of my sixtieth birthday, I can't help thinking how very pleasant it would be if the kindly fates permit me to go peacefully in my sleep after singing this song as a fond goodbye with good wishes to all; and with the thought, I think how foolish it seems to make such a wish.

However, my first three memories of life seem to me to more or less reflect the social history of my family through the twentieth century as 'modern' Indians; and the values and imperatives in its particular mix of east-westism that I laugh at as 'whiskey-sambar'. It's a transitional, confused state of cultural gipsyhood, with new ways of being as the terrain of daily life in which old attachments or affinities bloom only as sudden grace notes from a world I am not part of except in snatches, as a cultural tourist and not as a settler. At such times I am briefly but powerfully swamped by the particular smell of a south Indian temple, that dear, familiar compound of jasmine, roses, sweet basil, sacred ash, incense, lamp oil, burnt wicks, coconuts, bananas, sandalwood, ghee and *samagri,* the offerings to the sacrificial fire. It's a smell like no other. It is how our house would smell in childhood after Varalakshmi Puja every August on a Friday when I piped in Telugu, "*Ma intiki raave, Mahalakshmi,*" (Come to my house, Goddess of Good Fortune).

My parents and aunt, born in the 1920s, disdained and discarded caste distinctions and old taboos including in food and in the ritual segregation of women during their periods, euphemistically called *dooram* meaning 'distance' in Tamil, or 'out-of-doors' in English. My father ate meat at parties, I was allowed chicken sandwiches, shami kababs and egg salad in mayonnaise and when we moved in the early Sixties to Bombay and our trusted family doctor said I was weak and needed more protein, my vegetarian mother matter-of-factly arranged to make meat soup at home, advised by Mrs Khan, our neighbour on Pedder Road. This was our lifestyle in the 1960s and 1970s.

As for women's external freedoms to study and work, to smoke, drink, swim, marry, travel alone within India or abroad, go clubbing and dancing with 'suitable boys' in college or out to lunch with male colleagues if working, and wear Western clothes in suitable company at suitable places—dramatic external changes had taken place in these departments over three generations in my radically westernised 'Tamil brahmin' or 'Tambrahm' family.

Religion was viewed as an entirely private matter, distasteful if bruited abroad. There was an inner world and an outer world, mediated by strict codes of behaviour. It was vulgar to speak loudly and wholly forbidden to speak impatiently or impolitely to servants, elders and strangers. This did not stop the men of my father's family from swearing the most vivid and colourful oaths, of course, not permitted in women and children. Oaths and abuse were called 'the Fifth Veda' in that family, and like a great many things, were a male privilege. This is a proclivity that I later discovered I had inherited but naturally could not proclaim since nice girls did not use bad language; and being a nice girl, though a 'modern' nice girl as my family understood it, was the role awaiting me, which I was programmed for.

What my aunt Kanti and my parents chose to keep from their immense historical and cultural baggage was an essential simplicity, a lack of humbug, a love of learning, fine arts and good food and above all, Carnatic music. This was taught to me as "our true and only home" as my mother called it when I wanted to go out and play as other children did but had to stay home for the music teacher.

Perhaps because of my mother's presence through my childhood, I am the last person in my immediate family to have learned Carnatic music and to remain 'south Indian' in terms of language and culture. My younger brother and sister were offered the same opportunities and for a while, my sister did learn Bharata Natyam when we came to live in Delhi after my mother's sudden death. As things turned out, however, my brother is a north Indian and my sister an American, although they retain a taste for south Indian breakfast food like *idli* and *dosa*, coconut rice and 'poppadums', remember Tamil joke words and can decode simple spoken Tamil.

They have dim memories of the radiant mother we lost in 'the Kumaramangalam aircrash' of 1973, with the instinctive clamp-down of Tambrahm emotional reserve if they accidentally overhear a snatch of the songs that our mother liked from old Tamil films like *Paalum Pazhamum* and *Paava Manippu*. This is the expressionless shut-face of the breed that outs instinctively despite quantities of veal cutlets and steak au poivre.

My brother turned atheist while still a pre-teen and my sister, an American citizen, is nominally a Hindu. She married a Dane and Christmas is their big family festival. I can see from her Facebook posts that she sets up very prettily for Dipavali and lights nice lamps. Once, during a rough patch at work, she asked my father to "pray to south Indian deities like Venkateswara", which he teased her about for years.

It is not easy to determine my father's religious feelings nor would he tolerate intrusive questions. In terms of where his deepest emotions are invested, his children agree that his religion is sports and its churches

My sister's wedding at San Francisco City Hall.

are cricket and tennis. He subscribes to a couple of Hindu religious magazines from south India and used to send money both to the medieval shrine of the Sufi saint Gharib Nawaz at Ajmer Sharif in Rajasthan and to a Vedic *pathshala* or Hindu scripture school in the ancient temple town of Kanchipuram in Tamil Nadu. My brother's Muslim cook makes traditional south Indian vegetarian food for my father like *rasam* and *sambar* and his north Indian favourites like *paneer*. My father watched my brother set up winter barbecues on a Hibachi grill with clinical interest although he gave up eating meat many years ago.

He does not go to temples and only ever observed two Hindu rituals which he ceased to do in the new millennium.

One of these was the annual *shraadh* or lunar death anniversary ceremony for my mother. Back in 1991 while on a visit to my sister in New York, my father realised that it was time for my mother's *shraadh*. Instead of asking my sister to arrange for a priest and a *puja* or prayer ritual at a Hindu temple in New York, he slipped into St. Patrick's Cathedral, knelt in a pew at the back and quietly recited the Twenty-third Psalm. That was

My sister and brother at a barbecue at home in their twenties.

his *shraadh* ceremony for his dead wife and we thought he had done the right thing as a visitor in a foreign land, to just go to the nearest accessible 'House of God' and quietly pray in her memory. We thought she would have liked it, too.

When I happened to tell the tale among friends in Delhi, a more ritually-minded north Indian Hindu friend was startled enough to say that she thought it was "a little too practical" whereas the 'whiskies' of my acquaintance, westernised Tambrahms like us, thought it was an excellent thing to have done.

My father lives with my brother and they once fell under the 'parish' of a muscular young south Indian brahmin priest, a 'practising priest' or professional ritualist who had been to scripture school and also worked out at the gym. He looked like a film star when he took off his shirt to be properly bare-chested for south Indian brahmin rituals. He came precisely twice a year to my father. Once, for my mother's *shraadh* and again for Avani Avittam, which only brahmins celebrate in south India and all north Indian Hindus celebrate as the festival of Raksha Bandhan.

Avani Avittam is the day that south Indian brahmins,

in a link with the northern homeland left behind millennia ago, ritually change their *yagnopavit*, the sacred thread worn by the men of the three Hindu upper castes. There are different days for this ritual, according to which ancient holy book that south Indian brahmin men are ancestrally affiliated to—the *Rig*, *Yajur* or *Sama Veda*. For my father, a Yajurvedi, it occurred when Dhanishta, twenty-third of the twenty-seven nakshatra or 'lunar asterisms' that rule Indian astronomy and astrology, rose in the lunar month of Shravan, between mid-August and mid-September. Shravan was Avani in Tamil and Dhanishta, the constellation Delphinus, was Avittam.

This ritual had apparently gone on every Shravan for at least five thousand years for men of the priest, warrior and merchant castes. It was hair-raising in its intensity. To my child's eye, there was power, elegance and mystique in how my father and the 'practising priest' performed the ritual. The priest had to guide my father, who could have technically performed this ritual himself as a brahmin, but did not know how, for his family had gone over in the 19th century from the priesthood to modern professions. My father took off the old *yagnopavit* with a Sanskrit verse and put on the new one with another verse. Their contained, codified hand-movements were as concentrated as classical dance gestures. They were supposed to do the *prayaschittam* or atonement ritual as well and ask pardon, like Jews during Yom Kippur, for sins committed knowingly and unknowingly in the past year.

The ritual began with *rishi tarpanam*, the offering of prayers to ancient sages which was my favourite part to hear, followed by *agni-homam*, offerings to the sacrificial fire. 'Green gram' or cooked *mung* bean was the *neivedyam* or offering for this ritual and *payasam* of milk, rice and sugar was made in those homes where there was a wife who knew the drill.

As south Indian brahmin women had done for millennia before her, my mother made the traditional ritual meal herself for Avani Avittam, despite having a day job every bit as important as my father's and having to see three children off to school. She had a light hand and an instinct for tempering and flavouring her food just right and collected and read cookbooks like literature. Like my brother, my sister inherited this knack from her and cooks quail, duck, turkey, rabbit and game with ease.

One year in the US, she won a five thousand-dollar prize for the best recipe, her take on Thai-style chicken, in an all-America contest run by a popular house-and-garden magazine.

As a little girl I looked forward to the Avani Avittam ritual feast, to the saffron-scented, cashew and raisin-rich 'milk pudding' or the *payasam*, the crisp, light, salted rings of *vadai*, the fresh crunchy *kosmalli* or 'lentil-cucumber-coconut salad' as we'd probably call it in Indian cookbooks, the cool tang of the yoghurt *pachadi* that my north Indian classmates called *raita*, the dal and vegetables cooked together in a delicious mush called *kootu*, the tamarind soup of *rasam* mellowed with ghee, the lightly spiced yoghurt curry of *morkozhambu*, the gigantic fried discs of *appalam* or 'poppadum' in a special big, cunning tin that had a sieve above its base to let the last bit of oil drain off and thin, fresh banana chips. My mother planned it like a military operation and that's how everything got done. This home-made ritual feast stopped with her death and no priest expected to be fed by my father ever after.

If questioned about either the prayer in church or the change of the sacred thread or about just putting it away

My brother in front at his sacred thread ceremony.

unused in his cupboard until the next time, I am sure my father would raise an eyebrow at the impertinence. His wife, his religion, his business: absolute ownership. It is entirely his choice to do this or not do that. Who in the world has the authority to question him?

My brother, who was given his sacred thread at age eight, took it off for good and never performed a single ritual except to take part in the *shraadh* for my mother. In this matter, the millennia had come to a sharp full stop.

A puja at home on my brother's birthday.

This did not inhibit him, however, from activating the endogamous network to find him a pretty North Arcot brahmin bride, Nandini, and marrying her with the traditional rituals; or from choosing to name his son 'Advait' after the clan adherence to Adi Shankara's Advaita philosophy. After hearing his scornful views of brahmin ways for years, many of which we agreed with, this was an interesting development. My father and I exchanged fleeting glances but never spoke of it. This was their *putra shikhamani*, 'the son, the crest-jewel', as the ancient phrase went. I wish my mother could have seen this smiling curly-haired grandson and my sister's pretty daughter Anya across the seven seas.

However, change they never so boldly, the sticking-point for many Tambrahm men remains their basic preference for sons of the blood despite their attachment to a daughter or two. They would probably have their teeth pulled than admit it in the politically correct circles they invariably move in now. So their five thousand years look very different to me.

Every family has its own story no doubt and as a girl born to a Tamil brahmin family I too discovered the marrow-deep misogyny in the traditional patriarchal Indian mindset. At a theoretical level the Tambrahms, like other Hindu communities, set the Devi or prime goddess of Hindu mythology up on a pedestal to be worshipped as the sacred feminine but in reality discounted women unless they delivered the goods in their prescribed role as a service sector.

Drawn from preceding centuries, the wifely virtues recommended by the sixteenth century brahmin poet Goswami Tulsidas of Varanasi in his *Sri Ramacharitamanas*, Aranya Kand, Verse Four, went out

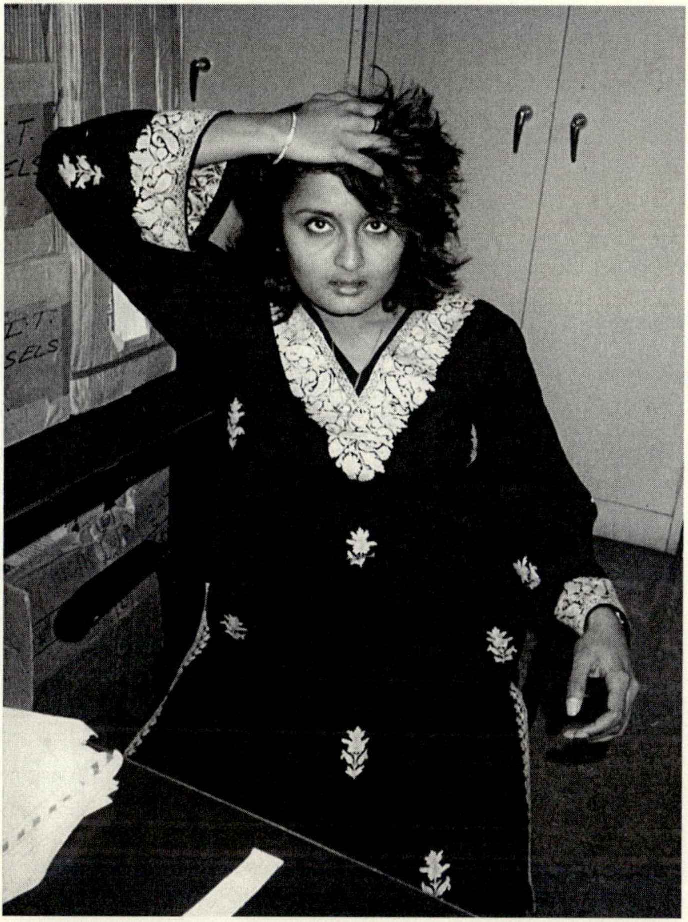

Not quite the formulaic good Hindu girl at twenty-two.

in his epic as advice for wives given to Sita by Rishi Atri's wife Anasuya: "Devotion of body, speech and mind to the feet of her lord, the husband, is the only duty, sacred vow and penance of a woman."

This job description had been detailed in the sub-universe of south India, too, in the thirteenth century, in a hugely popular verse. Written by the Telugu poet 'Baddena' or Bhadra Bhupala, in *Neeti Saara*, his treatise on morals, it said: "*Karyeshu dasi, karaneshu mantri, bhojeshu mata, shayaneshu Rambha, roopeshu Lakshmi, kshamayeshu Dharitri, shath dharmayukta kuladharma patni,*" meaning, "Like a servant in doing the household chores, like a minister in giving her husband intelligent advice, serving him food as lovingly as a mother feeds her son, as seductive and pleasing in bed as the celestial nymph Rambha, as beautiful as Mahalakshmi and as forbearing as Mother Earth: the woman who has these six qualities is the ideal married lady of the house."

This verse is very much around in south Indian brahmin families even today. Telugu brahmin women and Tamil brahmin women in world class, top corporate jobs have recited it sarcastically to me over a glass of Chardonnay or Lavagulin, smiles gone awry. We made faces then and touched glasses, saying, "Bash on, regardless," and "Confusion to the enemy."

Intriguingly, there is not one verse that I know of in the entire corpus of classical Indian literature, which details the virtues and qualities required of a husband. Nor could the well-known Sanskrit scholar Sundararama Dikshithar in that ancient seat of learning, Kumbakonam in the Kaveri Delta, tell me when I asked, in 2008. To his credit, he admitted it with unsparing honesty after spending a sleepless night trying to find one.

This entrenched attitude played out dramatically in the lives of the two women who influenced me profoundly, each representing an extreme; two linked yet different socio-historical trajectories.

One was Kausalya, 1929-1973, my mother, a dancer of note in her time, a well-received writer of novels and short stories in Tamil, the first woman officer in the Indian Customs & Central Excise service, a quiet rule-breaker who could do as she pleased in her conservative milieu not just because of her industrial-strength charm but because of her warmth and humility. She had everything—family support, brains, beauty, talent, the will to work, luck, success, popularity, an easygoing husband who was too content with life to be jealous or dominating, three healthy children, a series of nice homes, a flair for cooking and gardening, a dashing sense of style, an affectionate and sensible nature. She had considerable social, professional, creative and intellectual freedom and was registered to begin work on her Ph.D. in Bombay University with Professor Irani as her guide. Her fourth novel was being serialised in a popular Tamil magazine. She was liked by a number of people across caste, class and creed. She had it all. But one day, when not quite forty-four years old, her time ran out and she fell from the sky to a sudden, fiery death.

The other was my aunt Kanti, 1923-2000, the fatherless rebel, born to a wealthy family but fallen into wretched circumstances by the death of her charming but feckless father. She was brought up as a charity child, 'cabined, cribbed, confined' on account of being a girl and had to declare herself a pauper to Madras University to be able to study further. But she refused to be crushed by bad family attitude, poverty, sickness and professional setbacks. She taught Economics at Delhi University, went to Oxford, travelled in Europe, made wonderful, loyal friends at home, developed a rich, intense inner life, was invited, as an interesting person, to dine with Ambassadors by her friends in New Delhi, met the poor and the rich on equal terms and was staunchness personified in thought and deed. Though she suffered terribly, her spirit was somehow able to soar above the deep fault lines in Indian society.

Around these two women was a host of characters —grandfathers, grandmothers, aunts, uncles, cousins and friends—who were part of the tectonic social shifts that marked the first seventy-five years of the twentieth century, the general scope of this memoir, for my family of Tambrahms from the former Madras Presidency.

In attempting to convey something of these ordinary people who lived in extraordinary times and seized the chance to break free of suffocating old ways, each according to their bent and opportunity, I sincerely ask pardon for any errors and if anyone seems under-represented or overplayed. I can only tell the tale as I know it. And almost the very first stories of 'these old shades' that I heard were about my great-grandfather Raghavaiyya, my father's mother's father. He was the first person in our clan to drop his caste name, 'Aiyar', influenced by the modern ideas he had absorbed through

his English education. He did so in the 1890s and upset a number of people in his village and in his adopted hometown, Chittoor, now a part of southern Andhra Pradesh but in his time a lush, green part of the Madras Presidency, which ran along the eastern seaboard of India from Kanyakumari at the tip of the sub-continent to Ganjam in Orissa.

Raghavaiyya was perhaps merely being true to the brahminical type of the North Arcot region, an eccentric breed famous in the Madras Presidency as a law unto itself. The canny, careful brahmins of the Kaveri Delta further south laughed at them as the 'Sillies of North-Arcot', the '*Vada Arkaad ashadu*', for their enthusiasms, which were sometimes to their disadvantage. But their simple credo was, "How can it be wrong if *I* am doing it?"

It was this do-as-I-please ease that marked my father's amble into church just as it marked the doings of Parshuram Sastri whom my brother was named after. This ancestor on my father's father's side reportedly upset his peers in the late eighteenth century by engaging closely with the *mlechh*, or 'foreign barbarians' by translating the *Dharma Sastras* for the East India Company. I only know that he did so at their bastion,

My father and brother at ease in their unchallengeable skin.

Fort St George, which grew into the port city of Madras, renamed Chennai in 1996 by political whim.

Perhaps the self-assurance of these men came from the mists of millennia, from when their adventurous northern ancestors crossed over in the first wave of migration to the southern peninsula; from those tufted palefaces who could tell when the moon would 'eat' the sun in eclipse and knew stirring tales of gods and epic princesses who had raised the endurance bar to excruciating heights while in their blood rang the hard-edged consonants of their strange, strong language, Sanskrit.

Despite this romantic paleface bloodline from the *vadanadu* or northern lands, I was noticeably a coffee bean, a "sootball, not a snowball" as the Ottoman bride of a Nizam of Hyderabad called her baby. It upset people in the family.

In 1974, Ponni, my mother's mother, Ponnammal, meaning 'the Golden One' in Tamil, could not bear to see the tanned teenage legs between my school skirt and socks. Drawing me into my room, she shut the door and sat regally on the edge of my bed. She daintily pulled up her sari a little way, enough to show me a shapely leg with a trace of blue vein visible under translucent white skin. “Why are your legs so *brown*?” she asked me sternly in English. “See my leg, like alabaster.” She was not amused when I grinned, hugged her hard, saying, “What a pretty Paati,” *paati* being Tamil for granny, and ran off, pigtails flying.

I must have stifled a snicker as I left for it was her dead daughter, my mother, who had told me what to do, “Just listen, smile and go away.” Apropos of nothing, my mother had liked to cite Audrey Hepburn, whose ears “stuck out like Gandhi’s,” she said, “but look how she made an asset out of a liability with that haircut and those clothes, so stylishly gamine.”

I quite liked my café-au-lait skin tone but being “dark” in a light-skinned family came up almost as ritually as Avani Avittam. Vishali, my father’s ivory figurine of an aunt, enormous diamonds flashing in her ears, told me when I was eleven or twelve that great-grandfather Raghavaiyya’s skin was so pale and fine that when he drank hot coffee you could actually see the flush go down his throat. “Perhaps you could try lemon juice,” she added encouragingly.

My father's nicknames for me were The Miscegenation and The Throwback, to a "scuffle in the sand", he joked, between a dark-hued Unknown and "one of us" somewhere back in the ancestral line. His elder sister Kanti, a good many shades lighter than I but also categorised as "dark" on the clan palette, later said she would have dearly liked to slap my father for his line in humour.

She would also have liked to give "one tight slap," she fumed, to other ivory-pale old ladies of the clan who sat on polished teak swings in inner courtyards or verandahs, threading strings of flowers for daily worship and putting them away delicately in openwork silver baskets. "Is this Kausalya's daughter?" they would ask on our visits to Madras, "*Niron kammi,*" her complexion is below par. I would smile docilely, on my best behavior, waiting for squares of home-made almond *halwa* and *adhirsam*, little fried sweets that were, I discovered years later, the *gulgule* made for 'Goverdhan Puja', an ancient ritual honouring the tilled earth, performed by many north Indians including brahmins of the same *gotra* or ancestral lines as my father and mother, Vasisht and Bharadwaj.

The colour bar came up in Bombay, too, when I was about nine, and my mother was at work while I happened to be at home on a school holiday. The Hindi magazine *Dharamyug,* meaning 'The Age of Dharma', was doing a feature on Tamil brahmins in Bombay and a reporter and photographer came to the home of a Tambrahm lady in our building. The shoot was set up as a Carnatic music class and a few little Tambrahm girls were rounded up for it.

After telephoning my mother for permission, I got our housekeeper to comb my hair, and as told, put on bangles and my traditional skirt and blouse, the *pavadai-chokka.* We were arranged in formation at the lady's house on a grass mat as if at music class and the photographer looked through the lens. He pointed at me and said in Hindi, "*Isko hatao,*" remove this one. The Tambrahm lady said I could go, with the parting lament, "*Nee yaen onn'amma maari illay?*" Why are you not like your mother? So I took leave politely as taught and went home, back to my storybook, puzzled but not wounded.

My mother called after a while to check if I was safely back and said "Good," to my matter-of-fact account. She began to talk of something else and came home that evening with a new Enid Blyton; 'least said, soonest mended', no doubt. I forgot about it and it was only after my mother's death, when I kept going back to everything I could remember about my time with her that I realised what the *Dharamyug* incident had been about.

A melodramatic Hindi phrase now comes to mind about the patriarchy: "*Aap apne bheria chalaye mujh pe,*" 'you set your wolves on me'. But fair Kausalya had cued me to laugh it away, introducing glamorous Audrey Hepburn into the picture in a roundabout way and made it all so interesting, taking it to another level of discourse altogether. I realise now that this was counter-ideology by a smart woman with a pure motive, a mother who knew exactly what her daughter would be up against. Accordingly, she had fought the patriarchy from day one with its own weapon, the mind, making sure to never show her hand. She had trained me to deflect such sideswipes and attacks direct from breaking my skin and drawing blood and to do so from a position of composure, ensuring her daughter's sense of self in the little time she had before she vanished overnight. "My mother, the bushido master," I thought, pulling my tummy in. 'Dark' and fiercely protective Kanti had wanted to beat everyone up. What had they done to Kanti under her big smile and big *bindi*?

Recalling the stories about my great-grandfather of the fair, flushed throat, I cannot help thinking that wherever the courage to drop his caste name came from—and it was indeed a brave thing to do at the *fin* of that *siècle*, over a hundred-and-twenty years ago—Raghavaiyya was nevertheless an enormously entitled Hindu male who had the centuries on his side even in rebellion.

- *Two* -

I owe most of what I know about Raghavaiyya, my 'father's mother's father', to the oral histories I grew up hearing from my father's sister, Kanti. The rest comes from a marvelous recap written for me in the 1990s by my father's first cousin, Girija Karthikeyan, and from tales told by other relatives over the decades. I was teased in childhood about this interest in old family stories. "What happened, then?" was my refrain and the hounded adult would wail, "Help, the Shintoist wants another installment," or "Take her away before *himsa* happens," or oftenest, "Don't you have a nice storybook to read by yourself?" I would not call it 'ancestor worship', though, just curiosity. My mother said it was because I liked to '*eeshify*' as the Tamil slang went, to cling to people. Asking them for stories was my way of keeping them engaged.

Stories about happenings from 1900 to 1945

and occasionally beyond, centred on the house that Raghavaiyya built in Chittoor called 'Sita Sadan' that he named after his mother, Sitamma.

Raghavaiyya came from the village of Brahmadesam near Walajahpet, now in Vellore district, Tamil Nadu. This is in the larger domain of 'North Arcot', my father's ancestral region. Arcot, from *Aaru Kaadu* or Six Forests in Tamil was the key province of the Madras Presidency.

The Bay of Bengal lay all along Arcot's east while to its west was the Mysore Plateau. The Javadu Hills were Arcot's southern limit and its northern boundary was the outcrop of the Eastern Ghats called the Tirupati Hills. The river Palar cut Arcot into two. The region north of the river and south of the Tirupati Hills, a little over 19,000 sq km, was North Arcot, which contained ancient seats of learning and many old temples.

Arcot, like the rest of India, had a tumultuous medieval history. Alauddin Khilji of the Delhi Sultanate had apparently sent his general 'Malik Kafur' south in 1311 on a get-rich mission, leading to a local decline.

Thereafter, the Vijayanagar Empire, 1336-1646, centred in Hampi to the west, had improved Arcot's prospects for a while.

Aurangzeb had established one of his generals as the 'Nawab of Arcot' in 1692, as a reward for the general's conquest of Gingee Fort and the Nawab had made his capital at the *town* of Arcot. However, Arcot town surrendered easily to the Maratha attack in 1740. Some years later, in the middle of the eighteenth century, when the British fought the French in the Carnatic Wars and later, Tipu Sultan, in the Anglo-Mysore Wars, to win south India, the Nawab of Arcot became a British ally to counter his rival, Tipu, who was allied with the French.

It was the British who did the most for North Arcot. Despite their presence in Surat, it was Madras that was their first big home base in the sub-continent and that was where they spread out from to capture the rest of India. So complete and well-established was the British presence in the region that by the nineteenth century Kipling called Madras *'a withered beldame now'* and the British called it 'the Benighted Presidency' with the affectionate contempt of absolute ownership. They had every reason to be complacent. They knew perfectly well that its prosperity was their work; they had built it up brick by brick after having fought a succession of pitched battles for it. Arcot's most significant rulers before the

British had been the Pallavas of Kanchi, nearly nine hundred years earlier. The Pallavas had been audacious seafarers, exuberant temple-builders and patrons of learning in whose time many wandering Jain, Shaiva and Vaishnava poet-saints had enriched and strengthened the local culture. The region had been annexed later by the Chola kings of Thanjavur, from the Kaveri basin further south.

The ancient Pallava capital, Kanchipuram, was even older than the Pallava dynasty. It was mentioned as far back as 300 BCE by Panini, the Sanskrit grammarian, and eulogised in the Tamil Sangam or Academy Era epics of the second century CE, in the *Silappadikaram*, written by the Jain prince Ilango Adigal and in its sequel, *Manimekhalai*, written by his Buddhist friend, the merchant, poet and critic, Shattan.

In ancient lore, the Indian sub-continent was called *Bharatavarshe Jambudvipe,* 'the Land of the Bharatas, the Island of the Rose-apple', further detailed as *Aa Setu Himachala*, 'from Rameswaram to the Himalayas'. Seven *mokshapuri* or salvation cities were identified across it in ancient times, which still rule the Hindu world—Kashi or Varanasi, Avantika or Ujjain, Ayodhya, Haridwar,

Mathura, Dwaraka and Kanchipuram.

Of these, only Kanchipuram is in the south or the Dakshin, which the British anglicised to 'the Deccan'. No less than Mahakavi Kalidasa, the renowned Sanskrit poet of the fourth century CE had praised Kanchipuram in a Sanskrit encomium known all over India to the educated of various professions: '*pushpeshu jaati, purusheshu Vishnu, nareeshu Rambha, nagareeshu Kanchi*', 'the best among flowers is the *parijat* or 'night-flowering jasmine'; among men, it is Vishnu; among women, Rambha; among cities, Kanchi'. So the North Arcot region had been culturally celebrated since very old days, with Kanchipuram, Mahabalipuram, Sriperumbudur and the important temples of Tiruttani and Tirupati as pearls in its diadem. The last two were my ancestral temples, one Shaiva and the other, Vaishnava. Raghavaiyya's wife's ancestral village, Tandalam, lay between Kanchipuram and Sriperumbudur, which were known as '*ghatika sthanam*' or 'seats of learning' in Sanskrit across ancient Jain, Buddhist and Hindu traditions.

When the British won south India in the eighteenth century, they apparently rewarded their vassal, the Nawab of Arcot, with the title of 'Walajah', meaning

My ancestral deity, Kartikeya, at Tiruttani temple.

'most dignified gentleman' in Persian—an ironic title but seen from this distance, well-suited to the character of the people with its sarcasm smoothly wrapped and delivered, 'the needle in the banana' as the old Tamil saying goes. The Nawab, perhaps to turn the awkwardness of his situation to good account in the critical eyes of his subjects, who were wearied of being battered by the guns of the *parangi* or *feringhee* in war after war, took a loan from the British and with their permission, commemorated his new title with a new silk-weaving centre called 'Walajahpet'; '*pet*' or rather *peyt* from *peyttai*, meaning 'settlement' or 'where people live' in Tamil.

A portrait of Stringer Lawrence, 1697-1775, the 'Father of the Indian Army' once adorned the Banquet Hall of Fort St George, the British bastion from which 'Madras' began. It was he who used the Nawab 'Walajah' of Arcot for the advancement of the East India Company just as the Nawab used him to ward off Tipu and the French. A reproduction of that painting still adorns the foyer of the old Bangalore Club, which I loved visiting with my Bangalore cousins in my teens for a swim and a shandy, and enjoyed staying at in my fifties.

Portrait of Stringer Lawrence and Nawab Walajah at the Bangalore Club.

The Nawab, who seems to be held in a firm grip by the stout Englishman, looks rightly worried in this portrait, for he ran up huge debts to the British and eventually lost his territories to them. A later nawab was renamed 'the Prince of Arcot' by Victoria in 1871 and given a tax-free allowance called the Carnatic Stipends. Curiously, the 'Amir-e-Arcot' is the only 'erstwhile ruler' to legally retain his title and privileges in modern India and is accorded the rank of a state Cabinet Minister by free India's central government in its Warrant of Precedence. I found these larger histories very interesting because the political choices and educational endowments made by the Nawabs of Arcot benefited my family as individuals, enabling them to come out of medieval stagnation into the larger modern world.

Firmly under the British crown in 1866, Walajahpet, the silk-weaving town next to Brahmadesam, my great-grandfather's ancestral village, became the first modern municipality and *taluk* formed by the British in the Madras Presidency. It was also one of the first places to be connected by rail to Madras so it must have been quite easy for Raghavaiyya to go study in Madras and come home or go about sight-seeing in the holidays, which he liked to do. As the son of a locally renowned family of Sanskrit scholars, it was his unquestioned birthright to get the best available education and his family could well afford to send him to Madras. But there is absolutely no doubt that if required, the last paddy field and coconut grove would have been sold to finance his education, or the gold jewellery of the women, for North Arcot brahmin women usually had an *odyanam* or gold belt, whatever else they lacked.

It seems my great-grandfather graduated in Botany from Presidency College but then went on to the Madras Law College and thereafter set up practice in the town of Chittoor further up from Walajahpet, close to the pleasant hill resort of Madanapalli, famous for its mangoes and its British sanatorium, in the region known as Rayalaseema. Raghavaiyya had been sent to school in Chittoor in any case for the Chittoor Board High School was a fine old place, a grand colonial building set in nearly three acres of grounds, begun in 1854 by the British and generously endowed by the Arcot Nawabs (I have its centenary brochure from 1954, discovered in an old trunk).

The school had a robust tradition of producing properly-schooled Macauleyites and several famous south Indians studied there, like the first Lok Sabha Speaker Anantasayanam Ayyangar, educationist Kattamanchi Ramalinga Reddy and several important Telugu parliamentarians.

In later years, India's philosopher-president Dr Sarvepalli Radhakrishnan taught at the Chittoor Board High School and famous visitors included Theosophist Annie Besant, who visited Raghavaiyya's house, Sita Sadan; poet-politician Sarojini Naidu; and Nobel laureate Rabindranath Tagore, the last particularly admired in south India along with the religious and social reformers Ramakrishna Paramahamsa and Swami Vivekananda, as the Bengal trinity.

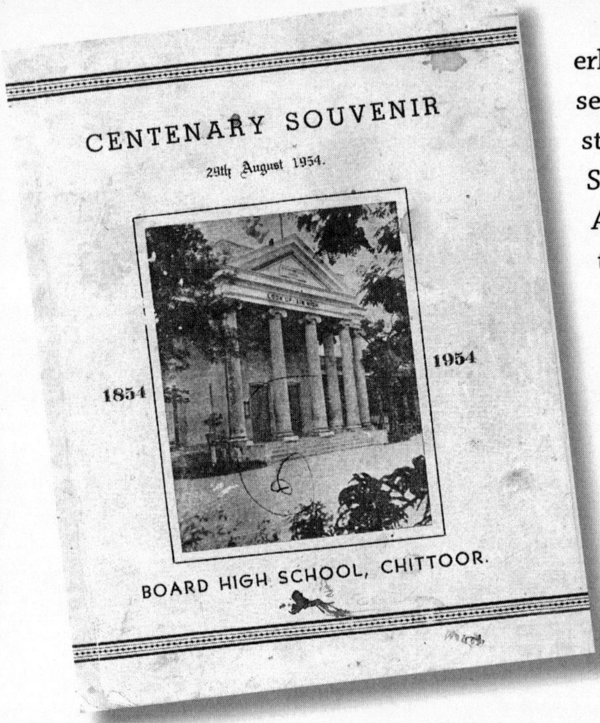

The Chittoor Board High School centenary souvenir.

Raghavaiyya's sons, grandsons and a son-in-law were also to become students and patrons of the Chittoor

Board High School and my father studied there, too. On a visit to Chittoor in the late 1970s, I was absurdly pleased to see the names of my uncles on the Board of Merit.

My father's favourite male cousin, C.V. Chandrasekhar, M.Sc. (Wales), had written with characteristic Tambrahm bluntness in the school's centenary souvenir, "District officials come and go…in the true spirit of democracy, we should not flatter district officials or their family to distribute prizes or preside over functions; these positions of honour should go to men of the town who have been brought up in the traditions of the school."

His elder brother, Dr C.V.L. Narayana, BA, BL (Madras), Dr. Es.Sc. Politiques (Geneva), Advocate, Supreme Court, New Delhi, had written of his "home that fostered a cosmopolitan outlook" and that, "If I had eschewed quite early the mentally cramping restrictions of caste, creed, class and colour which enabled me to travel widely and mix with people of various nations, it was due to my early associations with one and all in the school, no matter whether they were rich or poor, Hindu, Muslim or Christian." He wrote, too, of the long family association with the school from Raghavaiyya's days.

Since his village name was Brahmadesam and his family name was Cidambi, my great-grandfather's full name was 'Brahmadesam Cidambi Raghava Aiyar' in the traditional south Indian order: place name first, family or father's name next, personal name third and lastly, the family title, like Sastri, meaning scholar, or the caste name Aiyar that came from the northern word Arya. Arya had morphed from Aryar to Aiyar in the Tamil country, 'r' being the Tamil honorific at the end. Some Aiyar or Iyer men had chosen to use the generic caste name Sarma, Sharma or Sharman as their last name.

The Aiyars were Shaivas who worshipped Vishnu with equal ease whereas the Sri Vaishnavas, called Aiyangar, Ayyangar or Iyengar, were wholly dedicated to the worship of Mahavishnu from the time of the reformer-saint Sri Ramanuja in the tenth century. My great-grandfather changed his name to 'Raghavaiyya', which was caste-neutral whereas 'Raghava Aiyar' had differentiated him as brahmin. The story that drifted down the decades to my ears was that the ultra-strict brahmins of his ancestral village, Brahmadesam, did not care for Raghavaiyya's newfangled notions and politely suggested that he move to freer climes, not that he would have gone back to his village when primed to explore a new life.

Chittoor, a big, pleasant town, had a 'brahmin street' like any other place but Raghavaiyya did not choose to live there. Perhaps his reputation had preceded him and he was refused a place. My aunts and grand-aunts were silent about this possibility but it was long before they were born. Victoria had a few years to go then as 'Queen-Empress of India' and life in Sita Sadan was to prove very good, so that any silkily-worded unpleasantness at the Chittoor *agraharam,* or brahmin street, may well have fallen unregretted and unremembered into the dustbin of family history. Rather, and this seems more likely, Raghavaiyya chose to break away to expand his circle of friends, obtain professional freedom and provide easy access to himself as a lawyer by building a large street house, very close, in fact, to the Chittoor mosque.

The people of Chittoor spoke Telugu, Tamil, Urdu and English and lived on good terms with each other. My grand-aunt Vishali, Raghavaiyya's youngest daughter of the 'flushed throat' story, told me that if the children of Sita Sadan fell sick, Raghavaiyya's friend, the Maulvi Saheb of the Chittoor mosque, would come home and say Quranic prayers over their heads, "*Mantram sholluvaar*," 'He would utter mantras', was the way she put it.

In the usual Indian way of nesting a story within a story, I would like to add that this 'live-and-let-love' attitude went further in the next generation. Vishali's son, the film music director M.B. Srinivasan, brought home a Muslim bride, Zahida Kitchlew, Pundit Nehru having officiated at their wedding in New Delhi. 'Zaidi Ammi' as I called her, was a daughter of the barrister and freedom fighter Dr. Saifuddin Kitchlew of Baramulla, Kashmir. His ancestor Pundit Ram Prakash Kitchlew had converted to Islam and his grandfather, Ahmed, had moved to Amritsar in Punjab during the great famine in Kashmir in 1871. Zaidi Ammi's sisters were to marry and live in Pakistan and she was the only one to marry in India and move south. Her brother Taufiq, 'Uncle Toffee', a habitué of Teen Murti House Library in New Delhi, would visit me sometimes for tea in Delhi in the 1990s. Another sister, 'Rafoo Aunty', came to live with her in her last years.

M.B. Srinivasan, or 'Vasupa' as we children called

him, became a music director of note, particularly in Malayalam cinema, and introduced the brilliant singer Yesudas to the film world.

Vasupa, who had done productions with the revolutionary Indian People's Theatre Association (IPTA), had fought to get proper payment for the spot boys and the junior workers of the Tamil film industry and founded the Madras Youth Choir, seeking and adding the songs of the tribal communities of south India to the mainstream repertoire. I especially remember the lilting Badaga community song of the Nilgiri mountain region that I heard the choir sing on my visits to Madras. I remember Vasupa explaining counterpoint and harmony

Vasupa and Zaidi Ammi.

to me, making me sing all the English songs I knew to him and Zaidi Ammi and my cousin Kabir; and Vishali Paati laughing in surprise at how my old-fashioned repertoire took her back to her own schooldays in Chittoor.

The family's 'westernisation' had received a big push in Chittoor. Raghavaiyya often took tea with the English and since his practice was doing well, he had become one of the local notables, moving in Chittoor's 'first circles', in which the English District Judge and the English District Collector were the plums in the pie. He reportedly kept a fine balance in his dealings with the English, polite and friendly, close, even, but always maintaining a dignified distance that allowed no room for racial line-crossing.

By all accounts, Raghavaiyya had a realistic view of history. There was no denying that Hindu life had stayed frozen for centuries. Neither Hindu nor Muslim rulers had moved society significantly forward. Many brahmins, while at the beck and call of society for all rituals, had long abandoned their moral duty to set a good example to the society they were supposed to serve. Instead, they wasted their lives in minor sectarian disputes. A famously embarrassing instance, still talked about in my great-grandfather's time, was the petty fight between two warring brahmin sects at the eighth-century Parthasarathy Temple. This was in Triplicane in Madras, the ancient temple settlement that fell to the British in the eighteenth century. The two warring groups of brahmins had actually litigated several times to the East India Company about which group was entitled to recite certain ritual prayers. The British were the 'raja' now and to the 'raja' they had gone with their pleas and protestations.

Raghavaiyya recognised that the British had a more practical and useful notion of service to society than the brahmins. While the British were clearly profiteers, they had nevertheless improved life in their domains much beyond anything seen before. Instead of building grand palaces, temples and mosques or indulging in the vanity of extravagant and expensive tombs, they had built dams, schools, colleges, hospitals, harbours, railways and factories in their territory, the Madras Presidency.

In particular, the British engineer Arthur Cotton, 1803-1899, was a popular hero in the Dakshin for resolutely fighting his own masters, the East India Company, for many years, to build the great Godavari Anicut in 1847. He had even been summoned all the way to the House of Commons in London to justify this project to the British Parliament. It was the noblest deed of practical public service by any ruler in south India since the Cholas had engineered the Grand Anicut or *anaikattu*, meaning dam, on the Kaveri in the previous millennium. Arthur Cotton's Godavari Anicut had transformed the vast malarial plain of the Andhra districts into rich farmland. And now, more than a thousand years after the Kaveri Delta, the 'Guntur rice bowl' had become the other region in south India to grow three rice crops a year.

Cotton had built major irrigation works on the three greatest rivers of south India—the Godavari Anicut, the Krishna Anicut and the Kallanai Dam on the Upper Kaveri; and had drawn the plans for Vishakapatnam or 'Vizag' port. Raghavaiyya had been taken to see these marvels and particularly admired the grand Dauleswaram Barrage on the Godavari. To his mind it was a work of art that equalled and perhaps outshone even the great temples.

Moreover, the first modern general hospital in India was in Madras, built by the British in the seventeenth century. They had thrown it open to Indians in the eighteenth century after they had secured their presence in the Carnatic. The difference in public administration between the British and their predecessors was evident to the meanest intelligence. And they were undeniably men of courage and endurance. Just five hundred Englishmen had successfully held Arcot town for fifty-six days in 1751 against the French, and their enemies had withdrawn in confusion. Along with great works of civil engineering and town planning, the English had also brought exciting new scientific information to India, interesting literary and artistic forms, new intellectual ideas, discipline, order and method—everything that appealed to Raghavaiyya's own interests, inclinations and instincts.

These tremendous developments in the Madras Presidency were in unsung contrast to the history of the north. Barely seven years before the first Carnatic War the Muslim clergy in north India had seen their power eroded when Nadir Shah invaded Delhi in 1739, effectively wiping out the Mughals in all but name. The Marathas and Jats had gained strength after that.

The leading Indian Sunni cleric of the time was Shah Waliullah Dehlvi, who had translated the Quran into Persian and was influenced by the extreme views of

Abd-el-Wahab of Arabia. Much admired in the orthodox Sunni Muslim world, Shah Waliullah wanted Holi and Muharram banned in 'Hind' and the resurgent Jats and Marathas crushed. He wrote a desperate letter begging the up-and-coming Afghan warlord, Ahmed Shah Abdali, to "save Islam from the infidels". The consequent Afghan invasion had stopped the advancing Maratha tide at the Third Battle of Panipat in 1761. But it had not restored the power of the Mughals who were effectually over after Nadir Shah's expedition. Entrenched as the lords of the Carnatic and of Bengal, it was the English who had steadily advanced into the northern plains and taken Delhi over in place of the Marathas in 1803. They had, in fact, wrested India from the Marathas and French-fed Tipu, not the Mughals. The last Mughal was their puppet and lived in dirt and disorder according to English diarists.

The mullahs, in a desperate bid to restore the Mughal throne and thereby regain their own lost power, supported by the Maratha princes against the common enemy, had egged on the Mutiny of 1857 to drive out the English, which had begun as a mutiny and briefly raged as a civil rebellion. The Mutiny was supported by those parts of north India that were long unused to anything outside Mughal rule.

Explained to me by a North Arcot Muslim friend, this was apparently the fact of the matter, however much the Mutiny was romanticised by Delhi-centric nationalists in later years. The Madras Presidency had no reason to care. The advantages of British domination had made themselves evident in south India long before 1857 and south Indians were not going to risk their lives against the might of the *parangi* for the Mughals. In any case, the first mutiny had been theirs, in North Arcot, on 10 July 1806, when some disgruntled sepoys of the East India Company had mutinied at Vellore Fort, which had been built in the fourteenth century in the days of Vijayanagar. It had been taken over by Shivaji in 1677 and by the East India Company in 1768.

The British had tried to make their troops look more soldierly with a new dress code and a new turban and this had upset Hindu men, who wanted to retain their caste marks and ear-rings, and Muslim men, who wanted to retain their beards. Not only were these sepoys incited to revolt by Tipu's many sons and daughters who lived a luxurious life with large retinues to wait on them within

Vellore Fort after the fall of Srirangapatnam in 1799, but they were mocked at in the bazaar by Muslim fakirs who were sent by former associates of Tipu and reportedly in league with the Marathas of central India and the French at Pondicherry. Some sepoys, formerly soldiers in Tipu's army, had begun to abuse their new masters openly. The news of trouble brewing had been carried to the British by a fellow-sepoy, Mustafa Beg, for which the British later rewarded him with a subedar's pension for life.

Flustered by the news of the tip-off, the rebel sepoys had broken out in Vellore Fort earlier than planned by killing their garrison commander and another English officer and chased the other officers into hiding. But since nobody had a proper plan, the mutineers had then begun to loot the British quarters without any further thought. A quick dash to the rescue by Major Rollo Gillespie and his troops from Arcot town, fourteen miles away, had won the day for the British within eight hours and they had blown the captured mutineers to bits from cannons. The British officers who had ordered the new dress code had been recalled to England and their orders had been cancelled. Sir William Bentinck, Governor of Madras, had been dismissed. But the British had not taken out their fury on Tipu's family, only on the political rebels in their employ; and they had sent Tipu's family away to Calcutta.

Moreover, the south had not entirely forgotten that Aurangzeb 'Alamgir', the last of the six big Mughals, had attacked and looted Golconda and imprisoned its tolerant, benevolent sultan, Abul Hasan Tana Shah. In the Telugu-speaking lands once ruled by Abul Hasan, the smallest coin of virtually no value was contemptuously called an '*alamgiri*'.

After the spectacular failure of the Mutiny of 1857 in the north, many northern mullahs, frantic to retain influence at least over their community, had bitterly denounced English education and modern ways as 'un-Islamic' and as a straight ticket to hell, which had unfortunately succeeded in keeping any number of north Indians mentally walled-up against new ways. Nor had the local kings noticeably promoted the education of their subjects.

South Indians, particularly the brahmins, held no such historical grudge against the *parangi*. They had a longer, more dispassionate view of history. They had seen Hindu temples and kingdoms destroyed by Muslim invaders in preceding centuries, and equally, they had seen benevolent, learned Muslim kings. Long before the overland military incursion by Malik Kafur from the north into the south, south Indian Hindus knew and liked the peaceful Muslim traders who had come by sea to their coasts and settled amicably in their midst, marrying Tamil women with their consent and approval. The Hindus of south India had apparently given land for mosques to these friends who became family.

The south Indian Hindu tradition of scholarship was proudly upheld by Muslims and Christians. Had their lives overlapped, Raghavaiyya may have met and liked Justice M.M. Ismail, 1921-2005, of the Sufi town of Nagore in the historic region of Nagapattinam, who had graduated, like he had, from Presidency College and the Madras Law College. Justice Ismail, who became Chief Justice of the Madras High Court and the Governor of Tamil Nadu, was a learned scholar of the ninth century Tamil *Ramayana* by the poet Kambar. As president of the Kambar Kazhagam or Kambar Association, he organised many festivals of classical Tamil literature and was greatly admired in the Tamil world, though as a twenty-first century woman, I wondered what my puritanical great-grandfather had really thought of Kambar's drooling descriptions of Sita's physical charms.

By way of yet more perspective, south Indians had seen both their own *palayakars* or *thakurs*, called 'poligars' by the British and the invading Marathas fight and lose to the English. Vijayanagar, the last great Hindu empire, was long gone. Hindus always stopped at the exit of the Tirupati temple to admire the elegant bronze statues of Krishnadevaraya flanked by his two queens. He had ruled Vijayanagar from 1509 to 1529, lord of a real empire that had been greatly admired by foreign visitors. Just as Alexander had not ventured into the Gangetic Plain because of the Nanda Empire, Babur, the first Mughal, had apparently stayed north because of Vijayanagar. Krishnadevaraya remained an icon to south Indian Hindus who however accepted that rulers came, stayed for their allotted time and inevitably went their way.

I thought it probable that the Hindu view of time had helped my great-grandfather internalise these changes. The Hindu view of time differed from the linear Abrahamic view of it as a straight march from Creation to Judgement Day. The Hindus saw time as cyclical, from their observation of the diurnal round and the cycle of seasons, and had theorised it into epochs called *kalpa* and *yuga*. Nothing stayed forever, according to the Hindu view, except the Parabrahman, the Universal Soul, to whom all creation was a *lila*, a cosmic play.

Be they Hindu, Muslim or Christian, rulers were but *tableaux vivants* in a passing parade whereas Sanatana Dharma, the Eternal Law, which was Hinduism's name for itself, had outlasted everybody and everything. Shiva Nataraja at 'Thillai', his temple in Chidambaram, who was called Koothan, the Dancer, in Tamil and was believed "to dance always in the hearts of men," was merely the iconic embodiment of this ancient assurance. His earliest shrines had been built by the *perumtachchan* or master craftsmen noted in the Tamil Sangam literature of the second century.

Moreover, Raghavaiyya was a 'Smartha brahmin' whose personal philosophy of 'Advaita' was akin on several key points to the universalist 'Wahdat' of the Sufis, which may have explained his close friendship with the Muslims of Chittoor. Nor would he have failed to appreciate that it was the Arcot Nawabs who had saved the great temple of Srirangam from desecration by the French during the Carnatic Wars and donated garden grounds to it which were still called Nawab Thottam, the gardens of the nawab.

Also, it seems impossible that Raghavaiyya would have missed the Upanishadic resonances in the Book of Ecclesiastes in the Old Testament. The Jesuits had been around in south India for about three centuries and Ragahvaiyya had met and admired many in Chittoor and Madras, perceiving in them the same austerity, love of learning and elegance of prayer that marked him; Jesuits, saving their monkhood, were the 'brahmins of Christianity' and their sacred river, the Jordan, was easily recognisable as 'the Ganga of Christianity' while the life of Christ seemed curiously similar on several counts to that of Sri Krishna. Equally, Raghavaiyya had liked and admired his Protestant teachers at Presidency College and their strong work ethic that matched his own.

He was impervious to those Christian missionaries who ran down Hinduism as their religious duty. Hindus had their own armour and could keep a judicious distance from such people since mass conversions at gun-point or sword-point was not the British way, or the Arcot way, unlike that of the Portuguese in Goa or since '*Haider-kaalam*', 'the time of Haider Ali' in the south, which had been a byword in Tamil once for 'bad old days' and over time had come to mean just 'old days'.

Haider, a former soldier of the Mysore rajas and a territorial rival of the Arcot Nawabs, had sacked and looted the Tamil lands and neither Arcot nor the Kaveri Delta had reason to think well of him. Haider's son Tipu, a French ally, had tortured and forced many Hindus to the west of the Tamil country to convert to Islam. The Hindu kings of Kerala had appealed to the East India Company to deliver them, just as the Nawab of Arcot had allied with 'John Company' against Tipu and the French. It had been one set of adventurers against another in south India and the British had won, to the then genuine relief of many in the Dakshin. Certainly, Arcot preferred the phlegmatic British to Tipu.

Even the later racial divide with the British may have been seen as not a bad thing by many upper caste Hindu men in Arcot. The Hindu mainstream in the south was not a *purdah* culture as in the north nor had it ever needed to be. South Indian Hindu women did not cover their faces. Covering the head, too, was considered wholly inauspicious; that was only for hapless south Indian brahmin widows. Instead, the women of the south wore flowers and ornaments in their hair and held up their heads, their gait noticeably different from that of women in veils. Upper caste Hindu women at any rate were as safe from the *parangi* as they had been under the Arcot Nawabs.

Secure in his identity as a nineteenth-century brahmin man with centuries of scholarship and status behind him, and every prospect of advancement, living as he did in a well-administered region with almost every amenity then known to the modern world, in a snug pocket of an empire that nobody could touch, Raghavaiyya, had he known the Americanism, would have said, "What's not to love?" about the *parangi*. Accordingly, my great-grandfather welcomed the English as agents of positive change and progress and did not hold back from their language and culture. In fact he became a passionate believer in and enthusiast of English ways. Wanting to adapt English culture to suit Indian conditions, he took care to package himself as a man on the move.

We do not know what the *agraharam* made of

Ragavaiyya's phaeton, a type of horse-drawn carriage, or his car, a Ford. He wore English suits to court, topped with a neat, knife-edged turban that gave him an imposing air. His daughters told their daughters that he was the first Indian in Chittoor to wear a pince-nez, eye glasses with a nose clip instead of ear-handles, and to wear rimless glasses when those came into vogue. He was made a 'Rao Bahadur' by the Viceroy and attended the garden party at the Collector's House in celebration of the Delhi Durbar of 1911. But though he accepted the title, which was the equivalent of the OBE or Order of the British Empire, with every appearance of complaisance, he never used it. A modern professional degree was one thing but in his view a brahmin who had voluntarily thrown away the ultimate label, his millennia-old caste name, had no need of anybody else's hierarchical titles.

Sita Sadan had a *gadikhana* or stable-cum-carriage house nearby and a large back courtyard planted with herbs, flowers and trees. Raghavaiyya's devoted valet of years, Subbarayan, maintained his wardrobe, keeping a set of crisply-laundered *veshti-djubba* ready for visits by phaeton to Raghavaiyya's paddy fields at Pedda Kalavai,

My great-grandather B.C. Raghavaiyya.

his coconut plantation, his *maan-thope* or grove bursting with mangoes and the big, green pond where sons and grandsons were flung in to learn to swim with a couple of hollowed coconuts tied to their waists as floaters.

The family coconut grove.

Raghavaiyya's sons, my grand-uncles Sankaranarayana and Panchapakesan, were well-built and sharp-featured. It would have surprised and dismayed the entire connection had they not been so, given the careful genetic approach that had produced them. Mistakes were not tolerated in this important matter, as in much else, for North Arcot brahmins only married each other. Four North Arcot brahmin families of the villages of Tandalam, Pennathur, Calamora and Chethupet had exclusively intermarried for generations. This practice had gone on for centuries to preserve their blood line as expatriates from the northern homeland left behind eons ago. (This history of inbreeding was why my father called me and my sister 'Bonkers One' and 'Bonkers Two' while my brother was 'the Prize'). However, to expand the availability of partners in their regional circles, south Indian brahmins, including those settled in North Arcot, had tweaked the laws of consanguinity.

Back in the old homeland, a boy and a girl could not be married if they were *sapinda,* of common parentage, a term that came from the balls of rice (*pinda*) ritually offered to ancestors. According to the ancient Hindu lawgivers Brihaspati and Gautama, the offspring of five maternal generations and seven paternal generations are *sapinda* and cannot intermarry. Even the post-Independence Hindu Marriage Act of 1955 does not allow *sapinda* marriage. But the Act permits *sapinda* marriages "where such marriage is customary".

A south Indian brahmin was customarily permitted to marry his first cousin if the cousin was a 'cross-cousin', cross-cousins being the children of brother and sister, siblings of different genders. He could not marry a first cousin if that cousin was a 'parallel-cousin' for they were children of siblings of the same gender.

This seems shockingly incestuous to north Indian Hindus but then, they did not go away to far-off lands as expats in ancient times like south Indian brahmins did. Female feticide or infanticide, still so prevalent across north Indian communities and in some south Indian communities, was never a custom of south Indian brahmins. This was not out of extraordinary humanitarian concern for the girl child. Rather, they were too practical to waste or diminish genetic resources when cut off from the supply centre of their old northern homeland. They thought ahead of issues of continuity and comfort, the difficulties of travel in fetching brides from far-off regions, the difficulties that strangers would have in adjusting to the local language and lifestyle and vice versa; and took a collective decision at some point across their settlements in the south to expand their regional availability of partners through this method. The other advantage to this was the keeping of ancestral lands together in a family bloc. Such marriages are common even today among south Indian brahmins, especially the landed. As to which, my father's father's ancestral records going back many centuries are said to be with the pundits of Gaya Shirsha, in the realm of ancient Magadha in Bihar. But I do not know of anybody in living memory ever having gone there to find and update those records.

Inevitably, my great-grandfather Raghavaiyya had been married to the daughter of another North Arcot brahmin, a Subrahmanya Aiyar, originally of Tandalam village, now under Sriperumbudur taluk, Kanchipuram district, Tamil Nadu. The Tandalams were breaking away, too, from the old lifestyle to the exciting new world of the *parangi* and Subrahmanya Aiyar had migrated from the village to Georgetown, Madras-1, known less elegantly as 'Black Town' in the first expansion of Madras outside Fort St George in the 1640s. It was renamed 'Georgetown' only in 1911 to mark the coronation of George V as King-Emperor. Subrahmanya Aiyar worked as a *dubash,* from '*duvi-bhashi*', a person knowing two languages, as a translator for the British like his ancestor Parshuram Sastri.

Both the Cidambis and the Tandalams were apparently 'high-class brahmins' at the top of the top heap, Sanskrit scholars of long standing who were sometimes invited to be court pundits or ministers by local rajas and who maintained their own lands, establishments and libraries, playing liberal host to travelling scholars and sages and patronising temple events. They were offered every courtesy by the local lords, the *mirasdars*, *zamindars* and *palayakars*, and by the British, and sought after by other men of eminence.

Moreover, Tandalam Subrahmanya Aiyar was a brahmin among brahmins, of the highest class of 'Dikshitha', the person who gives *sanyas* or administers the ultimate Hindu vow of renunciation; and his daughter Tripurasundari was considered a catch even for a well-born, well-placed lawyer like Raghavaiyya. No brahmin woman was thought to need an education then, her appointed role as a service sector having been defined in Baddena's thirteenth century verse. But Subrahmanya Aiyar, being a whimsical North Arcot brahmin of the highest rank, could do as he pleased. Educating his bright, pretty daughter and showing her off in learned company was like an amusing hobby to him, much as training a parrot or mynah to speak would have been to a girl or woman. Tripurasundari was taught mathematics and logic and to read and write Sanskrit and Grantham, an old Dravidian script. She knew Tamil and Sanskrit very well and would cap quotations and argue politely but convincingly with her father and visiting scholars.

Nor were her domestic skills neglected. She was, according to my aunts, a very good cook who knew not only how to make regular food but also all sorts of special food and delicacies for every kind of festival and ceremony besides making nourishing food for invalids, for the pregnant and for those recovering from childbirth. She was taught to cut and sew well, to draw, paint and embroider, make exquisite *kolam* patterns on the floor and design sari blouses with leg o'mutton sleeves and ruffles of imported English lace in which to cut a dash at 'outside' events, meaning non-ritual gatherings.

Her seven fair and lovely daughters, of whom my granny Lalita was the sixth, were similarly taught their household chores and to cook and sew. They were also sent to a local school which had classes up to the Fifth for girls. Eminent teachers of classical Carnatic music like Chittoor Subrahmanya Pillai were engaged to teach the girls music without which no south Indian brahmin was considered complete or a properly brought-up person.

We can only imagine how heartily bored Tripurasundari may have been underneath it all despite her rich, kind husband, her brood of happy, healthy, beautiful children, her unshakeable status as the mother of two sturdy sons, her well-appointed home of which she was absolute mistress with no elderly female relatives to interfere, and produce flowing in from the fields and money from Raghavaiyya's clients.

But where was the life of the mind that once tasted could never be forgotten? There was no more Sanskrit and Grantham for Tripurasundari, who was no more the indulged daughter of a rich scholar in Madras living right in the middle of things. She was a married woman now with many children, a big establishment to mastermind, dairy accounts, field accounts and household accounts to be meticulously kept, workers to manage, ritual and social duties to prepare for, dress for and fulfill perfectly, dawn-to-dusk responsibilities, and all in pleasantly predictable Chittoor. No more being feted as Gritachi, the intellectual *apsara*, a celestial dancer of myth who was the classical byword for 'beauty with brains'. No more the company of clever, interesting men, their admiration and approval of her own cleverness adding sparkle to life but only the chatter of children and the company of well-born but uneducated housewives, now and forever.

It seems entirely natural that Tripurasundari missed Madras very much in the puritanical atmosphere of Sita Sadan. Her own family was both clever and rich and according to my aunt Girija, had "really lived the life of kings in the midst of Belgian mirrors and chandeliers." Tripurasundari's brothers and cousins were addicted to entertainment unlike the mentally open but personally austere and professionally focused Raghavaiyya. There were concerts, films and plays in Madras, visits to the beach to watch glorious sunsets or the monsoon clouds ride in, *nila paatu* or moon songs, meaning musical parties on the rooftop on full moon nights with the sea breeze blowing in from the Bay of Bengal, old established English shops like Oak's, Orr's and Spencer's, carriage rides along Marina Beach, 'the longest in Asia', new gramophone records from Sarasvati Stores and the latest English books from Higginbotham's on Mount Road, which her father would tell her stories from. Strangely, he did not think it necessary to teach her English; perhaps that was thought of as belonging solely to the world of men.

Wanting no doubt that her daughters should take their due place in the interesting world she had left behind, my great-grandmother compelled Raghavaiyya to marry two of their prettiest daughters to her Tandalam cousins in the Patnam or Town. Nothing else can explain her insistence. Raghavaiyya had the measure of his in-laws by then and tried to object. But Tripurasundari's wilful Tandalam blood was up and in any case, said the fastidious Cidambis, being a 'drama queen' came naturally to that theatre-mad tribe. Both marriages were phenomenal failures, although for different reasons, and the daughters came back in ignominy to Sita Sadan trailing their children behind them. One of these daughters was my father's mother,

Lalita. Tandalam men, it seemed, had been a law unto themselves beyond even the North Arcot brahmin usual.

- *Three* -

Back in 2007 on a personal visit to Chennai, I hired a cab to take me down the Madras-Bangalore Highway to find Tandalam village. We passed by the huge, gleaming Hyundai factory which brought back a half-remembered tale of a young Pallava prince sent out to marry a Korean princess in the ninth century. From which I remembered that *peengaan*, the Tamil word still in use for porcelain, came from Pyongyang, ancient centre of fine ceramics in South East Asia, where Tamil merchants sailed to trade over a thousand years ago. These merchants were important social figures, called Chetti, 'Seth' in the north, or Ethi and some were called Ethiraj, merchant princes.

Such musings turned to fine red dust when we found Tandalam, which looked desolate with no proper street and no proper houses visible to us unlike the villages of the Tamil countryside, which generally looked pleasant with a well-swept main street and houses painted fuchsia, royal blue, sunflower yellow and rose pink . Tamil villages had neatly-thatched huts, flowering vines on the *veli* or fence, *kolam* or geometric *mandala* patterns drawn outside even poor doors, chickens under high, round cane covers and a gigantic cardboard cutout of either the DMK leader or the AIADMK leader, depending on which party's turn it was to be in power, 'Delhi' being unable to take hold of Tamil Nadu since 1967. But Tandalam looked like nothing at all. We saw a few palm-thatched huts, a couple of dingy cement sheds with tin roofs, some straggling *aadu-maadu* or goats and cows and wide open spaces of rocky red laterite. Had all the action shifted to the engineering college set up in 1997? The village as a village seemed basically over unless we had made a mistake and this was not 'my' Tandalam at all.

It was all very confusing since the region had been minutely chopped up over time. The larger region of Arcot had been sub-divided by the British. What they had administered as 'North Arcot' was divided in 1989 into Vellore and Tiruvannamalai districts. Kanchipuram and Madras or Chennai, had together been 'Chengleput district' under the British but had become separate eponymous districts in the 1990s. However, Chennai

International Airport was not in Chennai district at all but in Kanchipuram district. Also confusing was that Walajahpet from where my great-grandfather had taken the train to Madras in the 1890s was in Vellore district but there was also a Walajahbad, the ancient settlement of Seevaram so renamed by the Arcot Nawabs, in Kanchipuram district.

So where was Tandalam then, of Sriperumbudur taluk, Kanchipuram district in northern Tamil Nadu closely bordering Andhra Pradesh? There was reportedly another Tandalam in Tamil Nadu but miles to the south at Kumbakonam taluk in Thanjavur district deep in the rice bowl of the Kaveri Delta, while a third Tandalam was promised to the far southwest near Neyyattinkara town, Thiruvananthapuram district, in Kerala.

"*Idhuya paaka vandhel, Madam*?" 'Is this what you came to see?' laughed the cab-driver and I laughed with him, in sudden sympathy with immigrants everywhere who romanticised their lost ancestral homelands. On a consolatory whim, I asked to be driven to Arcot town on the south bank of the dry Palar River to pick up thin-crusted, sharply triangular *samosas* from the Muslim tea-shops there. A *samosa* was a *samosa* and always welcome, however misshapen. But these elegant Arcot *samosas* looked like the ones my mother had got us from Irani cafes in the Bombay of my childhood and tasted even better, if that was possible. I had discovered them accidentally on another trip from Chennai when my cab made the big turn at Arcot for Kalavai. I was headed to Kalavai then to meet the Kanchi Shankaracharyas who were staying in their ashram there. I was offered traditional south Indian lunch after the meeting, and sitting cross-legged on the floor, eating rice with subtly-spiced pineapple *rasam* off a banana leaf, I had looked out at the coconut trees through the door and tried to imagine Raghavaiyya, Subbarayan and the great-uncles striding about in a similar setting at Pedda Kalavai or Kattamanchi, where my father's cousins had ancestral lands. I wondered if my father had ever come this way. He had not, as I discovered later.

North Arcot had fallen off my father's personal map as far back as the 1930s. His full name was 'Tandalam Srinivasa Narayana Sastri' but one day when he was a little boy, my granny Lalita had deleted both 'Tandalam' and 'Sastri' from his name. "Your father's personal name is enough for you," she had told him. Not knowing the whys and wherefores, he had grinned and gone off to play cricket topped and tailed of ancestry, 'S. Narayanan' for evermore.

Raghavaiyya's spirit must have approved, I thought, but Tripurasundari had been unable to contain her rage and disappointment at the catastrophic decline of the daughters who came back to Sita Sadan from their married homes in Madras. It was a personal failure and a public embarrassment that two of her prettiest daughters, handpicked by her as brides for her Tandalam cousins, should be so reduced. Her sympathy as a mother was subsumed in chagrin and she almost hated her unlucky daughters, turning particularly hostile to Lalita, the widow, now doomed by south Indian brahmin custom to be a social outcaste.

Lalita must have known exactly which Tambrahm women considered her presence unlucky and did not invite her to *pujas* or ritual worship ceremonies, to weddings and to the ancient ceremony for the pregnant to pray for a male child called *seemandham*, which had later acquired the social overlay of a 'bangle ceremony' in which *sumangali* women put new bangles on the wrists of the enceinte. Her own married sisters who were *sumangali*, meaning 'with husbands alive' would not eat with her as it was thought unlucky to eat with a widow. The patriarchal negation of centuries was embedded like a demonic microchip in the minds of women; to be executed by women on women who failed to bear healthy sons or did not succeed as wife material and as wives. It did not seem to me that much had changed a hundred years after Tripurasundari's daughters had been married like cows tied to the *yupa* or sacrificial pole in the old days of *yagnya*, the Vedic sacrifice.

The fact had to be squarely faced even now in the twenty-first century that in the Indian world, men were excused everything while a woman was no better than a tightrope walker at the fair, a *dambam-koothaadi*. One mis-step and she crashed to the ground. There was no safety net and no stretcher or ambulance. She had to get up on her own and find the guts to look everyone in the eye when her 'natural' protectors accidentally or expediently vanished or ill-treated her. There was nowhere to hide from this fact. The attitude of the joint family and thereby of Indian society in general to widows, orphans and unmarried women was openly discriminatory. Of course, there were honourable exceptions but not noticeably enough.

My sister escaped for good to America from Delhi in the 1990s, from the woman-unfriendly environment that she called 'Taliban Lite'.

But there was nowhere to escape to for a south Indian brahmin widow in the 1920s. The most difficult rite of passage from wife to widow was the head-shaving. Another woman, weeping, or silent in horror, would lead the new widow to the cowshed where the barber waited. The widow would be traumatised forever by that experience, humiliated by the touch of a strange man on her very head, which had been so proudly tended and crowned every day with flowers, never veiled inauspiciously, for that was only for widows, but held up to the sun, moon and stars as 'God' intended. She would awake sobbing at night on her grass *paai*, no more plump cotton mattresses, no sleeping husband nearby to wake for comfort, to save her from the barber's plundering razor that would return every month for the rest of her life to shave her head.

I wondered if there were those brahmin women who felt no pain and no humiliation, only the joy of liberation from having to bow to a despicable master. Women who did not mind that their foreheads would be bare of wifehood's red badge of vermilion powder or that their heads would be shriven forever of a wife's trophies of flowers and jewels. Perhaps they welcomed the barber as joyously as if he were a bridegroom and their falling curls were *akshada*, the lucky rice thrown at newlyweds by wedding guests. They may have worn the *jaavi*, the widow's sand-coloured cotton sari, as regally as *vairoosi pattu*, as though it were nine yards of wedding silk shot richly through with real gold thread, and marked their foreheads with sandalwood paste or ash in place of vermilion powder, released for good from Baddena's verse, although the price of freedom was dire.

But this was to speculate. The reality of the widow's lot was crushing. It had been thought through to the last detail and was organised and enforced to permit no escape. No wonder there were those who had actually preferred *sati* once, to burn themselves on their husband's funeral pyre, and this, too, had suited the joint family well. It was a tidy despatch of loose ends, oiled with false glory for procedural convenience. 'Ruthless pragmatism' did not begin to describe the great Indian family; and like their confreres in other regions, south

Indian brahmins had codified the precise methods of a widow's social exclusion.

I was frightened when I first saw a *mottai-paati*, a south Indian brahmin 'bald granny', on a visit to Madras in 1965. I began to notice more such women at Matunga in Bombay where my mother went to shop every few weeks for south Indian spices and vegetables. I could not get over it. Life as I knew it was on cosmopolitan Pedder Road, with a smart, pretty mother who went to office and the aunt who visited us from Delhi also working, also always beautifully dressed. The other women in my life were like Mrs Julie D'Souza, my favourite teacher at Hill Grange High School primary section, and all the other power-exuding, well-dressed women who taught at school, some in dresses or skirts and some in crisp saris. My mother's dear friend, Prema Raghavan, did not work and neither did most women in our building, but they wore nice clothes and jewellery. The *baais* who came to clean our homes were as pretty and bright in green, yellow and rani-pink saris worn with big *bindis,* glass bangles and strings of orange firecracker flowers in their hair that they called *aboli* in Marathi and south Indians called *kanakaambaram*.

My mother, her non-Tambrahm friends and their big daughters wore lipstick and nail polish, smelled nice, were always seen in pretty colours and had nice shoes and bags and stylish sunglasses. Their glossy hair was neatly coiled or put up in an enormous roll, or cut in a smart bob, or worn long with a 'Sadhana fringe' like the actress, and a bandeau. They wore silk or chiffon saris with a string of jasmine or rosebuds pinned to a smooth chignon when dressed up to go somewhere. As a little girl, I was in utter awe of these women. They seemed like queens and princesses, marvellous, beautiful, clever beings. Who and what were these other bizarre persons, creeping self-effacingly around?

Chancing upon a *mottai-paati* was like what seeing a 'freak' in the old circuses must have been—an unnatural, incongruous and ghastly sight. A *mottai-paati* was a human being stripped of her entire identity as a woman and as a person, condemned to walk apologetically on the fringe of society, the very sight of her dreaded as 'unlucky', unwanted at any joyous or 'auspicious' event. It was living death.

I asked my aunt Kanti about them on one of her visits and she told me the gist of it in spare, short sentences, that some women had been like that since they were little girls or in their teens and twenties. This discovery was a terrible shock. How could my ancestors have invented this form of torture for their own women? My scholarly, learned brahmin ancestors? How could I ever like them now, for this, and for what lay behind the slap that was my first memory of life? But how could I reject them completely either? My mother had been born to one of these men. She was married to one of them. Why had nobody saved these women? Was all of society part of the plan? Other girls dreamed of becoming dancers, pilots and film stars. My fantasies were that of a *piriki*, a coward. I wanted great strength like Phantom and magical power like Mandrake in Indrajal Comics to keep away I knew not what.

Avvai, the feisty old Tamil poet had said "There are only two castes, men and women." I knew several sayings and verses by her since childhood from my granny Ponni. What would Avvai, the Tamizh Thaai or Tamil Mother have said about this terrifying sight? I was too young then to fully understand the situation but knew that I was in the presence of something very wrong and very sad.

I could not articulate these confused thoughts to my mother and felt guilty about the immense dislike that had begun to grow in me for my male ancestors and relatives and my dread of the male specie in general. Thankfully, there was no *mottai-paati* at any home we visited in Madras but there were many to be seen around in the 1960s and 1970s. I would look down to hide the instant tears whenever I saw one. If my mother was nearby, she would unobtrusively hold my hand while I struggled to regain my composure, which had to be done, for that was our inexorable law of self-restraint, *adakkam*. She probably understood what I was going through but could not take on the exhaustion just then of explaining gruesome social history in further detail. In any case, restraint was bred in the bone. My mother approved of the aristocrats in the French Revolution who had played piquet, a card game, in the tumbrel on their way to the guillotine. That, too, was *adakkam*. She reinforced the lesson by paraphrasing from *The Jungle Books*, which I loved: "We, of one blood, we do not cry."

Our family at Pedder Road in Bombay with my sister on the paai.

It is a comfort to me in the twenty-first century that my granny Lalita refused to have her head shaved and that her brothers did not insist, despite the protests within the family and from other brahmins in Chittoor and Madras. Lalita was barely twenty-six when widowed, with three of five children surviving, of whom the eldest, Malati, did not last the first year of Lalita's widowhood. My father and his sister Kanti, 'Sami' and 'Leelu' to the family, were the two children left to her.

Lalita begged very hard to be allowed to study so that she could eventually get a job as a teacher and support her children. But Raghavaiyya's liberal, progressive outlook that had broken free of caste and creed man-to-man was not wholly imbibed by his sons when it came to a widowed sister. It was 'thus far, and no further'. Lalita's husband's family had abandoned her when her husband died. Her brothers kept her painfully dependent.

Lalita's torment as a widow grew worse in Sita Sadan, her own girlhood home. When the Periyaval or Elder Shankaracharya of Kanchipuram visited Chittoor, he said he would grant Lalita *darshan* or audience only if she shaved her head. Lalita refused, saying she had discarded the *pottu* on her forehead, her flowers and jewellery and

The Maha Sannidhanam or Shankaracharya of Sringeri on a visit to my grand-aunt's house, 'Gowri Kumar' in Chittoor.

that was enough. Her mother Tripurasundari flew into such a hysterical rage that Lalita and her children were sent away to a house nearby until the furore subsided and Tripurasundari had calmed down enough for the widow and orphans to return to Sita Sadan. And neither Lalita nor Kanti showed up when another formidable

Hindu religious personage, the Shankaracharya of Sringeri, visited Chittoor and graced Lalita's married sister's house with a visit. I had a picture of that visit and it made me shiver with its implacably privileged patriarchal aura.

With these sights and stories burning in my head, I went calling for *The Indian Express* in 2000, the year Kanti died, on the Kanchi Kamakoti Peetham, headquarters of the Shankaracharyas of Kanchipuram. I had interviewed the current 'pontiff' in Delhi in the late 1990s on "*What Hindus Hate about their Faith*" and he had given me reasonable, progressive answers.

Despite my rejection of so much else and contrary to everything that had built up in me, I was unable to resist the deep tug of ancestral attraction to Kamakshi Amman at Kanchipuram. The *Kamakshi Suprabhatam* to the goddess intrigued me. The 'wake-up prayer' to the 'Universal Mother' at Kanchi demanded like a child that she should make it a good morning for us, '*kuru suprabhatam*'.

When I arrived at the Kamakoti Peetham, the daily worship of Shiva as Chandramaulishwara, the Lord as Moon-Bearer, was about to begin, to be performed by the Shankaracharya himself. Long ago, the Sultan of Golconda, Abul Hasan Tana Shah, had put it in writing on a *firman* or sultan's decree, on three copper plates, that the revenues of Melupakka village nearby should go 'in perpetuity' towards the worship of Shiva as the Moon-Bearer at the Kamakoti Peetham, for this very *puja*.

The copper plates were in the collection of the Peetham and the Shankaracharya liked to distribute the Archaeological Survey of India monograph on them to as many people as he could. How well the men were able to transcend religious differences when they chose. Every interfaith meet I had gone to was peopled by men spouting clichés on peace and brotherhood. But they had invariably closed ranks against women.

I shook my head at myself. I was turning into a full-time fulminator. I was tired of being a nice girl, tired of always trying to be a better person than I was, but was too much of a *piriki* to be 'bad'. How had Lalita endured it?

Meanwhile, a group of women seated in the *puja* court were chanting the *Lalita Sahasra Naamam* from which Raghavaiyya had named my granny. This was an incandescent Sanskrit hymn to the goddess composed by Adi Shankara, on whom Lalita's father-in-law, T.S. Narayana Sastri had written a vast, scholarly work in 1916.

Leading the chant sat a *mottai-paati*.

I felt half-mad with grief for her and for Lalita, who should have reigned as the queen of her own home but had been reduced instead to being a poor relative, an indigent hanger-on. How could her own mother have turned against her when her life went so horribly wrong? Lalita had been married to her mother's second cousin, Srinivasa Sastri. A Tandalam mother and a Tandalam husband had let Lalita down. Who were these awful people? I never wanted to know.

I went back to Delhi from Kanchipuram, rage mounting in its familiar, exhausting cycle since the day I had heard scraps of Lalita's story from my aunt Kanti. It was Lalita who had suggested the name 'Renuka' years before my father married, should he have a daughter one day, and when I was born, and my father had mentioned it, my mother had agreed at once. My mother had a musical laugh but when I laughed, it was like *kottai-paaku*, said my father, like areca nuts rattling in a box, just the way Lalita had laughed. "The laugh of a

Lalita at twenty-five.

free, blithe spirit," he said. I no longer laughed like that and wondered how Lalita had been able to. Despite the driblets of information, I knew little of Lalita's actual thoughts and feelings for Kanti had burned her diaries and letters when she died, well before I was born.

What was left of Lalita except the beautiful diamond ear-rings that Tripurasundari had given her when she was married? They were now mine.

Years ago, Kanti had wanted to have them thrown into the Tirupati *hundi*, the vast collection box at this ancestrally-affiliated temple whose seven hills were the old northern boundary of the Tamil country and now lay in Andhra Pradesh.

"It seems one of the stones has a *dosham*," said Kanti uncertainly to me.

"I don't believe in unlucky specks," I said. "If all things are made by 'God', how can anything be 'unlucky'? Did you know that J.B. Haldane said that God had an inordinate fondness for beetles?"

"Don't wear that flippant mask with me," snapped my aunt. "I thought you were religious."

I made a big show of sighing deeply. "I need the idea of 'God' for a personal handhold through my troubles," I said. "But I don't buy superstition, only the nice symbolic stuff. Why don't you just sell them and donate the money to charity? Since when did Tirupati matter to you?"

"They have gone from mother to daughter for four generations, for almost a hundred years, I couldn't possibly sell them," fretted my aunt.

"So God's bin is your dumping ground?" I asked, interested by this cultural reflex. She looked hard at me as if about to slap me again. "Will you wear them if I give them to you?"

I looked back, my ever-ready eyes smarting. Wear Lalita's own ear-rings as a gift from Kanti?

"Is the Pope Catholic?" I said, trying not to spoil the moment with an unlovely sniff.

My aunt had also asked me to take away an old prayer book, which I had hurriedly thrust on a back shelf to see later.

Driven by some unclear impulse, I dug it out for a look. It was a battered old edition of a long Sanskrit prayer to the Devi as Kamakshi, the 'Love-Eyed' Goddess of Kanchipuram.

On the flyleaf, in Devanagari script, was an inscription in Hindi cast like the start and the finish of an unwritten letter: '*Mere priyatam Srinivasa*', 'My beloved, Srinivasa' and '*Tumhari priyatama Lalita*' 'Your beloved, Lalita' followed by 'June 1952'. It could have been written by a lovesick teenager, not by a widow of many years in her middle age.

I knew Lalita had died on 26 June 1953 at the Dehradun Civil Hospital. Kanti had taken her to Dehradun for a holiday and Lalita had fallen very ill and slipped away silently into the night. Her son and daughter had steady, respectable jobs by then and her long wait to see them securely established in life was finally over. "She seemed to let go of life, then," Kanti had told me. My father had rushed to Dehradun from Bombay where he was then posted and they had watched through the night as Lalita breathed her last.

Both in their early twenties and strangers to Dehradun, which was then a very small town in the forests of the Himalayan foothills, they had asked the hospital to help them arrange to cremate Lalita. Unexpectedly, a young Tamil brahmin couple living in Dehradun had come to know of it and stepped forward, arranging everything for the orphans and helping them through it all until they could take Lalita's ashes to immerse in the Ganga at Haridwar. These angels were Mrs Visalakshi Guha and Dr Subramanian Rama Das Guha of the Forest Institute. They were yet to become the parents of the modern historian Ramachandra Guha.

Lalita had been married on 30 June 1915. The inscription in her personal prayer book barely a year before her death could only mean that my grandmother had loved my grandfather all her life despite everything that had happened to her. It also meant that Kanti, who had suffered deeply on her mother's behalf and loathed her father's family for abandoning Lalita, could not bring herself to burn this very personal artefact in which a constant heart had overflowed just that much. It was everything. How could I have put the book away in my bag with just a word of thanks and a quick look at the cover without looking inside and turning over the pages that minute, that very second? Why had my aunt held back from ordering me to look? It was too late to tell Kanti what it meant to see Lalita's own words.

Maybe, just maybe, there were points to my grandfather Tandalam Narayana Srinivasa Sastri. He had died of 'consumption' or tuberculosis when my father was two and Kanti, six. There he was in his wedding

Lalita and Srinivasa Sastri on their wedding day.

photo, all of eighteen, with his girl bride of thirteen. At that point in time, on their wedding day, they had only thirteen years ahead as a couple. I suddenly wanted to put my arms around the doomed pair.

At the very least, and because it was the law of natural justice to hear the other side, '*audi alteram partem*' as great-grandfather Raghavaiyya might have said, I began to piece together the stray shreds of information on Srinivasa Sastri that had slipped through the Cidambi omerta. It was not disloyal if Lalita had loved him.

- *Four* -

Born in 1897, Srinivasa Sastri, called 'Cheenu' at home, was six feet tall and had qualified as an advocate by the age of nineteen from Madras University. The eldest son of a famous father, he led a generally pleasant life, though prone to catching chills. An easygoing sort, he never minded being despatched on escort duty if a country cousin came to Town and would good-naturedly take such visitors under his wing.

They dashed about to plays mounted by the famous theatre group 'Suguna Vilasa Sabha' of which Srinivasa was an active member. I had grown up hearing my father and Kanti snort "Suguna Vilasa Sabha" if I pouted or threw a little tantrum to push my limits, it was a term between them that took me years to decode.

The Suguna Vilasa Sabha, a Sanskrit term for 'quality circle', had been founded in 1891 by a group of theatre enthusiasts led by a gentleman called Sambanda

Srinivasa Sastri's boyhood home on Coral Merchants' Street, Georgetown.

Mudaliar. It began in a building on Thambu Chetty Street in Georgetown, next to Armenian Street, where the Armenians had a fine old church, and Coral Merchants' Street where my grandfather's family lived.

The *sabha* or association shifted in 1902 to the Town Hall, called the Victoria Public Hall. It specialised in Shakespearean drama, the plays translated into Tamil by its inner circle of well-educated members, including prominent lawyers at the Madras High Court in Bentinck Building. Senior British administrators came to its shows and the *sabha* often donated the gate money from its productions to charities. Srinivasa and his cousin may have seen *Amaladityan* (*Hamlet*) or *Virumbiya Vithame* (*As You Like It*) or *Jwalita Ramanan* (*Romeo and Juliet*) or *Sarasangi* (*Cymbeline*). The last, with its stolen brothers, secret marriage, inheritance issues, wicked stepmother, betrayals and disguises, had apparently been a Georgetown family favourite. Anything melodramatic was jeered at as "*Sarasangi*" by Kanti. It was another code word between her and my father.

Srinivasa and his protégé must have rumbled by tram from Georgetown to Chennai's oldest quartier, Mylapore, to look at its temple, the Kapali Kovil, its *gopuram* blazing with pink, green and yellow gargoyles and godlings, before surrendering to the black-and-white wonders of Madras's first cinema hall, the Electric Theatre on Mount Road or its second, the Gaiety Theatre, or perhaps at the Lyric, that had opened in 1913 but burned down the next year.

They may have set about choosing finely-checked saris in ochre and sienna or a shade of viridian called *Ramar pachchai* or 'Rama green', for the ladies at home, from Sampoorna Sastri's select shop on North Mada Street off the Kapali temple, or another just like it. Kanti had told me it was a very old and famous shop where she bought south Indian saris in traditional designs when she had a bit of money.

Srinivasa Sastri may have bought Peek Frean biscuits and tins of Rowntree's Cocoa for the cousin's children at Spencer's on Mount Road. This absurd family love of cocoa at bedtime had continued well into the nineties with me, replaced by tea and Kashmiri *kahva* only as I got older, but I still liked having a tin around. Spencer's was "the finest shop in the East" in Srinivasa Sastri's time, a grand red and white 'Indo-Saracenic' sprawl whose facade looked more like a church than a shop. Inside was a fairyland of fine things.

Perhaps the last time that the fine merchandise of the world had so spilled over on the Coromandel Coast was in the days of ancient Poompuhar, called 'Kaveris Emporium' by the Greek geographer Ptolemy. Puhar had been swallowed up by a tsunami as reported in the second century Tamil epic, *Manimekhalai*. And Mylapore in its earlier locale by the sea had been called "the potent city, Meliapore" in the *The Lusiads* by the sixteenth-century Portuguese writer, Camoens.

I was enchanted to discover in the definitive book on Spencer's by Madras's own particular historian S. Muthiah that my two worlds of north and south India had met in this historic emporium. The complicated electrical wiring had been done in 1907 by a Punjabi gentleman who had migrated to Madras. His son was the Test cricketer A.G. Ram Singh, 1910-1999, who had written his name the south Indian way as 'Amritsar Govindsingh Ram Singh'.

The cousins would certainly have gone on to Higginbotham's enormous book shop, built in 1844, not only to buy books for themselves but perhaps also to buy story books and picture books from England for the cousin's children. That is what my father and aunt did compulsively, buy books all the time, for books were a necessity, not a luxury. In the mid-1950s, my father, a young revenue officer in Bombay, had taken a government loan to buy a motorcycle. With the money in his pocket, he had stopped as usual after work to browse at the Strand Book Stall in 'Fort' and his money was gone. When my mother married him, all he had was a large wooden bookcase and a bucket and mug. Kanti had told me that Srinivasa, too, had run up huge bills at Higginbotham's.

The cousins may have well gone to Burma Bazaar to look for a carved Shanghai cane for a great-uncle or fine-toothed Jessore combs from East Bengal for the older ladies who were very particular about their toilette. If there was serious diamond-buying to be done, they would have called on Srinivasa's elder Tandalam cousin, Kalyan Sastri, who was skilled in *ratnapariksha*, the assessment of precious stones, and was often asked his opinion on diamonds, especially by Peter Orr & Sons. The Orrs were Scottish watch-makers whose partners in 1843, the Gordons, had been trading in Madras since 1792. The firm had operated from a grand Byzantine-style building on Mount Road since 1849 and Kalyan Sastri's keen eye would have ensured that the cousin got the best stones he could afford.

With a play, a film, a concert and some shopping done, the country cousin would have been put on a bus back from Parry's Corner, with his silver *kooja* filled with water and fluffy *idlis* wrapped first in pink lotus petals and then in banana leaf before being neatly parcelled with a shred of banana fibre. If the cousin had come to Town to buy a car, Srinivasa would have whisked him off at once to Addison & Co on Mount Road and he would have gone home in state.

The cousin probably went home thinking what a nice fellow 'Cheenu' was although instead of the brahmin's topknot he wore his hair English-style, parted on one side and longer on the other. Most scandalous of all, he wore a *djubba-veshti* , the south Indian 'kurta' and 'sarong', only to a temple or a concert, generally preferring a light English suit, a crisp white shirt and a grey cravat, the only concession to south India being a fine diamond stud in one ear, the *kadukkan,* without which no south Indian brahmin man of that generation felt dressed.

Srivivas's older Tandalam cousins liked to play

billiards at the Cosmopolitan Club, which had begun in 1873 and relocated to Mount Road in 1882. It was where the anglicised 'Indian elite' went, the Madras Club then being a white preserve. The big cousins took Srinivasa along and he was hooked, spending more time playing billiards than in looking for work. They also introduced him to superbly aromatic Light of Asia cigars from Spencer's own factory at Dindigul. Later, when Srinivasa was about to be married and wondered if his bride would protest, the cousins laughed, quoting Kipling, "A woman is only a woman, but a good Cigar is a Smoke."

One particularly tall, handsome cousin was very taken with the popular singer Gauhar Jan on her visit to Madras in 1910. She had based herself in Thambu Chetty Street in Georgetown and Kanti had told me when I was about seventeen that he followed Gauhar Jan about and "threw a gold *mohur* at her feet for every song". "Did your father go, too?" I asked. Kanti paused. "I don't like to think he did," she said. "But did he?" "Yes, he must have, he was very close to that cousin," she said.

I had seen this great-uncle at his son's home in Poes Garden, Madras, on our visits south in the 1960s. He was very tall, fair and handsome even in his old age. I remembered that unlike the old aunts, he said nothing about my complexion but looked me up and down clinically and pronounced, "Long neck and tapering fingers." He was also noted for saying, "The only way to tell if a woman is attractive is—strip her." Kanti had heard him say that and muttered something about "wife-swapping vulgarians".

"What?" I said, "How debauched. So are you your father's child?" "How dare you say that?" she snapped. "It's a logical question," I said. "Not us, I believe it went on only in some families," she said firmly. I must have looked thoughtful because, in defensive clannish reaction, she looked down her aquiline nose at me and drawled, "Your mother was a talented girl, my dear, but we were the aristocrats." "You sound like your brother," I said, recovering, for two could play, "He's always telling me that my mother came of 'good yeoman stock'."

The big Tandalam cousins also took Srinivasa back to the ancient Vedic habit of eating meat. An English meal followed the sacred formula of soup, chicken or fish, meat, potatoes and vegetables, and pudding, often a lemon or mango pudding in tropical Madras, followed by coffee and cognac. The cousins made a hobby of schooling

Srinivasa in English habits much as Subrahmanya Iyer had schooled his daughter Tripurasundari in mathematics, logic, Sanskrit and Grantham. Srinivasa apparently enjoyed it all very much, coolly breaking every taboo with aplomb.

A hanger-on of the big Tandalam cousins, whose proper name I never discovered, but only heard of as 'Chuppunni' entered the picture. By all accounts, Chuppunni was the classic ne'er-do-well who preyed on foolish boys with a bit of money. He introduced Srinivasa to placing bets on the horse races at Guindy, which he found exciting.

"*Aadhe ghorey pey, aadhe laurey pey,*" I had said experimentally to Kanti, searching for a summary. Delicately put, this was Hindi for 'Half his money was squandered on horses and half on women.' My aunt's Hindi did not include such phrases and I had to translate. "Where do you pick up these revolting expressions?" she bit out. "It's only language and it's only to you, I don't talk like that outside," I said hurriedly but I had crossed the line and she withdrew into icy aloofness. I felt mildly aggrieved. Who had mentioned these things in the first place? My aunt had not liked it when my brother questioned her on these matters in his teens, resenting his habitual mocking tone, and had told him sharply not to malign her father. As for the horses, an incident from childhood suddenly made sense.

When I was in Class Six or Seven in Bombay, I was captivated by the pictures in the papers and badgered my parents to take me to the Mahalakshmi Race Course, which they flatly refused to do. "Why can't we go?" I demanded to know. "Ten-year-olds can't go," said my mother. To block further entreaties, she said sternly, "Your father and I are both revenue officers. Do you want us to get a bad name? In any case, we are not interested in the races," and that was that. If it was an *adakkam* issue, there was no more to be said.

My mother was amused but not entirely pleased by this request. I accidentally overheard her discussing it with my father and saying, "It's your bad blood coming out." "Ah, your little bourgeois soul objects, does it?" he laughed back and I scuttled away, ashamed to have eavesdropped. But after a minute I plucked up the nerve to go back and confess that I had overheard. I regret to say that this was only partly because of my ongoing training in being a nice girl. The need to know what 'bourgeois' meant was very strong, too, and since I did not know how to spell it, I had no hope of finding it in the Concise Oxford Dictionary, which my father had trained me to look at every time I came across a new word. My mother, never losing the opportunity to knock another nail in, said, "See how much nicer it is to have nothing on your conscience?"

Despite these hurdles, I loved looking at horses and actually learned to ride just to put the attraction to rest, as did my sister at Captain Kundan Singh's on Safdarjang Road in New Delhi. I knew I had the worst seat and hands in the Commonwealth and eventually stopped but I still liked to look at horses. Had my grandfather actually liked horses or just the odds of the race?

Between billiards and races and plays and bookshops, Srinivasa only ever came home to sleep those days. There had been nobody at home for years to take a particular interest in him, no mother to wait up anxiously and nag him to work instead of wasting his time with his fun-loving cousins. "No Cidambi-like person," was left unsaid by my disapproving sources. Srinivasa's mother, Sitalakshmi, a Mylapore girl called 'Chinna' at home, had died when he was barely five.

Chinna's father's name was Palathope Subba Aiyer and I knew absolutely nothing about him. Who was this great-great grandfather exactly, I wondered. 'Palathope' meant 'jackfruit grove'; the Madras region had once been rich in orchards and groves, well-watered by the rivers Adyar, Cooum, Palar and Kosasthalaiar. Several areas in 'Town' took their names from the flowers, fruit or trees that had once flourished in them. For instance, besides Palathope, there was Mambalam from '*maampazham*' in Tamil, literally 'mango fruit'; Vepery, which would have been 'Neem Talao' in Hindi, probably an *aeri* or pond that had *vepe* or margosa trees around it; and my favourite, Triplicane, which was the wholly mystifying anglicisation of '*Thiru-Alli-Keni*', meaning 'Sacred Lily Pond'. As far as I knew, 'Palathope' was Vedanta Desikar Street in the heart of Mylapore and I longed to know something about this great-great-grandather's life and antecedents but had no way of knowing. It was all gone with Chinna, who had floated in like a butterfly through the Tandalam window and flown out, unremembered and unsung, her coming and going of no consequence

Srinivasa Sastri as a motherless boy in Sundari Sadanam, Georgetown

to anybody, it seemed. Srinivasa must have missed his mother. I could not bear to think of it. His father had married again and the second wife had had enough on her hands with her own small children while Narayana Sastri was wholly absorbed in his next *magnum opus*.

The only personal tidbit I had heard about my great-grandmother Chinna was that she had a lot of pride, "*Chinna'kku orey garvam*", or rather she had a lot of self-respect. She hated asking her scholar husband for money because he did not respond at once and she found it demeaning to keep asking. Once, when she absolutely needed to buy the children something, it seems he had felt in his pocket and handed her a four-*anna* coin. Chinna, who had worn a real *kaashu-maalai* or necklace of golden guineas at her wedding, looked at it and, very improperly for an obedient nineteenth century Hindu wife, flung it at her husband's already retreating back. It fell to the floor just a pace or two ahead of his feet. Ignoring this communication, my Tandalam great-grandfather had stooped to pick it up and walked out indifferently without missing a step.

"How mean, I don't like Narayana Sastri," I said in disgust and my father, passing by, looked at Kanti who had just told me the story. “Well, why not?” said my aunt to my father, who shrugged and walked away as indifferently as my great-grandfather must have done. Kanti had no more to say on Chinna.

I asked my mother, the oracle, about it, “Amma, why did that Thatha not give Chinna Paati money when she needed it?” My mother said in a light, bored voice, “I don’t know and I don’t want to know,” at which unmistakable snub I backed off and never dared mention my great-grandmother Chinna again although I wanted very much to know more about her. I was embarrassed on her behalf and embarrassed by my great-grandfather’s paltriness. All that book-learning and scholarship was of no account if your name was hurled to the floor like a four-*anna* coin by your grand-daughter and the son of your eldest son did not care. What price, *putra shikamani*? This sorry tale came back when I encountered medieval Hindi couplets, the *dohas* of Kabir, Rahim and Tulsi. A *doha* by Kabir pointedly said, ‘*Pothi padh-padh kar jag mua pundit bhayo na koi. Dhai akshar prem ke jo padhe so pundit hoye*’; ‘Nobody ever grew wise by reading a great many books. By ‘reading’ two-and-a-half alphabets of love does one grow wise.’

But could I really condemn Narayana Sastri, 1869-1918, given the influence of his father? Narayana Sastri's father, my great-great grandfather Tandalam Ramakrishna Sastri, had been an old-style scholar who had studied the Vedas and Sastras under an immensely learned guru, Pundit Ishvara Jatavallabha. My great-great grandfather had apparently excelled in studies and been given the title '*Veda Nipuna*', meaning 'Veda Expert'. He had vastly preferred the pleasure and detachment of study to domestic duties and managed to evade being married until he was forty. But Ramakrishna Sastri's guru pressured him to marry his own daughter, Sundari, who was ten years old to her bridegroom's forty. I felt absolutely wretched to think of it. 'In due course' as they say—when, dear Lord, I wondered—Sundari had produced two sons and two daughters. My great-grandfather was the younger son.

Ramakrishna Sastri had died a dramatic death. He was expounding the *Skanda Purana*, about our ancestral deity Kartikeya, while being fanned by my great-grandfather. He had stopped suddenly in mid-sentence, gazed amazed at a vision that only he could see and uttered, "*Har Har Subrahmanya,*" meaning 'Praise the

Lord'. His eyes stayed wide open but blood began to spurt from the crown of his head and that was it. I could see it happening. I could imagine my great-grandfather's shock at his father's extraordinary death and partly understand his own retreat into study. But, said my Cidambi side, why had he married, only to ignore his wife and children? Was it because of the ridiculous old Hindu belief that only a son could save a man from the hell called '*put*', hence '*putra*' for son; the 'deliverer from *put*'? A wife was merely the socially endorsed conduit for this, then, of no earthly use unless she produced a fine, healthy son and fulfilled her ritual duties as a *griharani*, the 'queen of the house'. Traditional Hindus did not see their wives as precious individuals; any woman would do to keep their lives going. What were these enormous, self-serving lies invented by my ancestors and taken up so happily by the rest of society?

Certainly, nobody at 'Sundari Sadanam', 16, Coral Merchant's Street, Georgetown, would have objected to Srinivasa's original dissipations of books, music and theatre. These were certified and legitimate family obsessions. Notwithstanding Kanti's dreadful story, my great-grandfather, who called himself 'Tandalam

Sankara Narayana Sastri' was actually a formidable scholar. He knew eighteen languages—eighteen including Greek and Latin and had a vast personal library besides an enormous and valuable collection of palm-leaf manuscripts. His elder brother, T.S. Venkatasubba Iyer, was a Sanskrit scholar himself and also a highly successful criminal lawyer in Madras, acquiring the sobriquet 'Indian Norton' after Eardley Norton, who was a very famous criminal lawyer of the time from an old English family of Madras and greatly respected by the Indian National Congress.

It was Venkatasubba Iyer who had set up and succeeded in Town first and at some point sent for his younger brother to have him educated. When T.S. Narayana Sastri arrived in Madras as a tall, lanky twelve-year-old, he knew Tamil and Sanskrit but no English. The Town cousins promptly called him '*Nattakaal* Narayanan' or 'Spiderlegs' and 'A-B-C-D Narayanan'. But Narayana Sastri did everything that he came to do and got his *sanad* or licence as High Court vakil at extraordinary speed, specialising in civil cases while his elder brother took on the criminal cases. However, his heart was in Tamil and Sanskrit literature and ancient Indian history;

and with an elder brother to comfortably lean on, he researched and wrote one book after another which celebrated ancient heroes in a flood of Tamil, Sanskrit and English, making good use, among other sources, of the Government Oriental Manuscript Library, Madras.

I was interested to discover that T.S. Narayana Sastri had published a history called *Kings of Magadha* in 1917, just before his death. But Kanti Sastri was gone and S. Narayanan did not know of it.

"Did he really?" said my father, when I told him. "I wonder why."

"Appa, if your ancestral records are in Gaya Shirsha, of course your grandfather had an interest in ancient Magadha."

"Probably," said my father. He changed one sports channel for another and I knew it was my cue to disappear.

There appeared to be a mystery about T.S. Narayana Sastri's collection of manuscripts that had apparently vanished after his death, described in a book published by Motilal Banarsidas in 2001, called *The True History and the Religion of India: A Concise Encyclopaedia of Authentic Hinduism* by Swami Prakashanand Saraswati.

The title was not encouraging. At one point it cited T.S. Narayana Sastri's book on Magadha and claimed that his manuscripts had obviously been stolen by the British to keep Hinduism down. A conspiracy theory about my great-grandfather's personal library? How very odd.

I Google-searched the author and was horrified to find that he was a typical '*babaji*' or pseudo-swami, a convicted child-molester on the run from American law since 2007. This was being tainted by association, indeed. As far as I knew, it was a close relative who had taken away any number of Narayana Sastri's precious books and manuscripts from my grandfather Srinivasa to whom they had been bequeathed. My grandfather had fallen very ill and this close relative had had the run of his house and apparently made good use of the opportunity, according to Kanti. Could this person have actually sold the books and papers to a 'British agent' to be destroyed? Was he, in fact, the agent? Or just a thief?

"I don't know and I don't want to know".

I remembered my mother's words and wished I had never opened the Tandalam can. I had run into one of my father's estranged Tandalam cousins once in Madras. This person, sarcastically called "sweet coz" by dead

Kanti, had informed me that the Tandalam nickname for my dead mother was "the holy Kau". "Witty," I'd said politely to this backhander.

Why was I poking about in what did not concern me? It was absolutely horrible to think that Narayana Sastri's theory in 1916-17 that many things in Hinduism were older than the British said they were, based on his study of old manuscripts collected over the previous twenty years, had been cited by a criminal *babaji*. I was mortified by the random angle. Like Aunt Ada in *Cold Comfort Farm*, I could now say that I had seen something nasty in the woodshed.

However, my great-grandfather's most popular work, which had made him famous, seemed unexceptionable for its time. It was a seven-act play in Tamil called *Bhoja Charitram*, which was first presented by a literary society-cum-theatre group called 'Vidwan Mano Ranjani', Sanskrit for 'the pleasure society of pundits', on 16 April 1898 in Georgetown. It seems the public loved it. It was successfully re-staged several times in Madras and 'the Hindu Social Club' of Rangoon had presented it at the Jubilee Hall, Rangoon, on 1 May 1915. The book was reprinted thrice.

The play was set in ancient Malavadesa or Malwa, Madhya Pradesh, and its hero, Prince Bhoja, was sent by a wicked uncle to fight Pulakesi, mighty king of the Andhras. Drawn from old Sanskrit stories, *Bhoja Charitram* featured princesses, dowager queens, a chalice of poisoned milk, an about-to-kiss-but-sternly-holding-back moment, quite mountains of *masala*.

Dr Sarvepalli Radhakrishnan had walked several kilometres to see *Bhoja Charitram* as a young man of Madras and greatly liked it, he told Kanti years later in Delhi when he was President of India and discovered her antecedents, particularly that the Tandalam ancestral temple was at his birthplace, Tiruttani. Kanti, who taught Economics at Miranda House, Delhi University, had been taken to meet him by his son, the historian S. Gopal, and his wife.

My great-grandfather had also written far and wide including to the then Maharaja of Tehri-Garhwal to track and gather ancient manuscripts relating to Adi Shankara. He had published *The Age of Sankara* in 1916, the first book in English on the ancient Hindu reformer, and made over its royalties to the Kamakoti Peetham, to the Shankaracharyas of Kanchi. His work had been ridiculed by some scholars and upheld by others.

I had been asked by Penguin India to write a 'Life of Shankara', which I did not complete for various reasons, chiefly the exigencies of earning my *dal-roti*. I wished however that I could take a look at my great-grandfather's book. Naturally, my father did not have a copy and the Kamakoti Peetham did not have a clue to its whereabouts on their premises. So much for ancestral adherence.

One April day in 2004 in Delhi, while waiting by the India International Centre's car-hailer for my driver, I got into a sudden conversation with a woman standing next to me. It turned out that she was another great-granddaughter of Narayana Sastri's and had a copy of the book. We spoke for barely two minutes. But Shankari very kindly made a spiral-bound photocopy and had it dropped home before going abroad soon after. I never saw her again but I greatly cherished the gesture and the warmly-inscribed photocopy. Our meeting had a surreal quality to it as though the mists had parted for a moment and the book had dropped through.

I was taken one day in the Noughties to the house of a distant North Arcot relative within the fabled grounds of the Theosophical Society in Madras, to admire a gigantic Thanjavur-style painting, all goldleaf and gesso work. It was a vision of the Gayatri Mantra as a goddess incarnate that great-grandfather Narayana Sastri had had one night and promptly painted in the Thanjavur style, for he had apparently been an artist as well as a scholar and was particularly known for his images of Shiva Nataraja and the Devi. This resplendent painting of Gayatri stood grandly in its original rosewood frame in the *puja* room of this house. They told me that somebody from Narayana Sastri's family had given it to them from his *puja* room after his death.

I wondered who had and felt a momentary pang of attachment. But a line from a Hindi poem by Harivansh Rai Bachchan came to mind, '*jo beet gayee so baat gayee*', 'what is past, is past'. I sank to my knees, put out the ring finger of my right hand to dot *kumkumam* on my forehead, did a namaste to the painting and left, glad for the glimpse. That was enough. A Sanskrit *sloka* about the sacred feminine was my direct legacy from great-grandfather Narayana Sastri that he had composed to the Devi. Kanti had taught it to me when I was very little. His sloka went, *vande mataram ambikaam bhagavateem vani rama sevitaam*

kalyaneem kamaneeya kalpalatikaam kailasa natha priyaam

vedanta pratipaathya maana vibhavaam vidwan mano ranjaneem

sri chakraanchita bindu peetha nilayaam sri raja rajeswareem

Salutations to mother-goddess Ambika, who is served by Sarasvati and Lakshmi,

Who is the beautiful, auspicious wish-giving tree, the beloved of the Lord of Kailash,

Whose lethal weapon against the forces of darkness is the Vedanta, who delights the minds of the learned,

Whose abode is the mystic Sri Chakra yantra, who is the Queen of Queens.

Fine words, and sung by no less than two absolute stars of the mid-twentieth century Carnatic firmament, Chembai Vaidyanatha Bhagavathar and G.N. Balasubrahmanian, 'GNB' in Carnatic lore. I had found their old recordings of my great-grandfather's verse on YouTube while searching for renditions of my childhood prayers. A Sanskrit scholar said, "What poetry!" of this undeniably beautiful verse. But, I thought, my heart hardening against Narayana Sastri for his neglect of Chinna and Srinivasa, words were cheap given the yawning chasm between theory and practice.

I wished instead that I could have sensed the presence of great-grandfather Raghavaiyya at the Theosophical Society. When his son Sankaranarayana had come back from studying at Trinity College, Dublin, Tripurasundari's Tandalam brothers and a great many other brahmins had forced Raghavaiyya to make his son undergo the *prayaschittam* or ritual atonement and purification ceremonies for having gone outside the country. Was it not enough that he had come home safely in the thick of World War One, that his ship had dodged the German U-boats? And what if he had come home with "an Ll.D (landlady's daughter), not an Ll.B" as the joke went those days, a prospect seriously feared by those Indians who sent their sons abroad? The social pressure to make his son perform *prayaschittam* had so disgusted and humiliated Raghavaiyya that he had turned Theosophist in reaction. Tripurasundari had made peace with him and had even accompanied him to meetings at the Society.

Raghavaiyya had built himself a meditation room of coloured stained glass on his roof and when Annie Besant visited Chittoor in 1917, she had come to tea at Sita Sadan. She had gone up to the meditation room with Raghavaiyya, where they had both sat awhile in silent contemplation. I had seen this room on my visit to Chittoor in the late 1970s and had briefly closed my eyes to try and see what it felt like. Many years later in Delhi at the house of Kanti's friend, Devaki Jain, American feminist Gloria Steinem had told me that she, her mother and her grandmother had all been Theosophists, who were in fact one of the originators of the modern feminist movement.

However, none of these impressions and recollections added up to a better picture of my grandfather Srinivasa. Kanti's one memory of him had been that she used to run to him as a six-year-old and he would swing her up in the air. My father, who was only two years old when his father died, naturally could not contribute a personal story. Lalita had held it all in and did not speak much of her married life when she was mistress of her own house in Linghi Chetty Street, or was it Thambu Chetty Street, in Georgetown, which she could not keep because there were a few payments left and Srinivasa had been too ill to go out and find work.

Perhaps if the rich Tandalams had rallied around a bit and helped her keep her house, she could have rented a portion to a 'respectable' family and kept her independence and her dignity and that of her children? But how could a pretty young widow of twenty-six live alone without '*purusha thonai*', a legitimate man around? Oh no, that was against 'family honour' in 1929. They had sold the widow's roof over her head, paid off Srinivasa's doctor's bills and sent the suddenly destitute Lalita back to her father's house for good, her three surviving children in tow. They had let her keep her diamond ear rings which were from her Tandalam mother's mother. Lalita had pawned her other jewellery to have a little money in hand and her brother Panchapakesan, who became a Judge of the Madras High Court, 'Panju Mama' to her children, had redeemed it quietly without telling Tripurasundari. Oh, the shame of it, for Lalita. What had cut her the most, according to Kanti, was that very close male relatives of my grandfather whose task it was to light his funeral pyre, had said it was "too cold" to go to the cremation ground and someone else had officiated. *Finis*.

The two definite plus points I had on Srinivasa Sastri was that he loved animals and he was a wonderful singer. Kanti had his RSPCA medal engraved with his name for his service to the cause, and as for the singing, I had that, too, from Kanti, who had it from Lalita. It was Aunt Girija, Lalita's sister's daughter, who finally wrote me about Srinivasa Sastri with Cidambi precision and brevity: "Srinivasa was not very interested in law. Young and handsome, he spent most evenings at the Suguna Vilasa Sabha, a premier stage for Tamil drama. He was very intelligent and if he had taken to the law seriously, he would have done very well. He had five children. But his failing health brought about his end very soon. Raghavaiyya liked Srinivasa very much and had high hopes of him."

Well. That was as damning as it could get. A charming wastrel, *c'est tout*. Lalita's family were fully entitled to their opinion, having had to pick up the pieces.

I was back where I'd started. Why blame the

Lalita with Srinivasa Sastri.

Tandalams entirely for not helping Lalita, when it was her husband's job in the first place to provide for her security? Why had he carried on like an entitled young prince and not used his intelligence? What was the point of being born to a privileged family with every advantage, if you did not repay life with work?

It was a wholly "holy Kau" moment. At this juncture, I felt far removed from my father and Kanti. I felt terrible for them. But I also wanted to escape their unhappy past and not transfer their baggage to my head like a karma coolie. I wanted to belong only to my nice, normal mother, to her brightness and beauty and not to these walking wounded, these damaged waifs of history. But I had had no escape from Tandalam "bad blood" after Kausalya's death.

Aunt Girija's letter went on, "Though so young, Lalita was stoic and had determination and grit. She became part of Sita Sadan lore. Her children and Raghavaiyya's other grandchildren all grew up together. Lalita was a voracious reader and within her short span, she read the complete works of Tagore, Bankim and Sarat Chandra Chatterjee. She read all the classic English novels. She closely followed the struggle for Independence even though she could not take part in it. Lalita used to tell us stories about Nandanar, the dalit devotee of Lord Nataraja. She had no caste distinctions whatsoever. Lalita had mastered the works of Sri Ramakrishna Paramahamsa and Swami Vivekananda. She had such a serene face that one of my cousins used to call her 'Sister Nivedita'."

The senior Cidambis had not shone either despite Raghavaiyya's example. After nearly twenty years as a well-behaved widow, Lalita was blamed for Girija marrying Karthikeyan, a non-brahmin, and for her nephews marrying non-Hindus. The powers at Sita Sadan did not properly consider the effect of the changing times they lived in on their children or the ideas of a new social order of justice and equal opportunity that electrified the Indian air in the 1940s, the idealism and the excitement of the time. Afraid for their jobs in the aftermath of the Great Depression, anxious about what would befall them if the British left India, the uncles took it up readily when a disgruntled male relative started a smear campaign against Lalita as "the source of all evil ideas in this house" since an unprotected woman made a handy scapegoat. There had been an ugly row and my father, barely a young adult then, had abused the cousin who started it and taken Lalita away for good from Sita Sadan to cheap hired lodgings. My father never spoke of it. Neither did Kanti. No Cidambi person wanted to speak of it.

Lalita seemed not to have looked back. She had stopped my father from joining the Army with his best friend, Krishnaswamy Sundarji, which had disappointed my father deeply. He had joined the Hyderabad Agricultural Service in 1948 instead, after taking a B.Sc. in Agriculture from Bapatla University, where he went to get a professional degree after his 'gentleman's education' at Madras Christian College. That had come to grief in his third year after a brahmin lecturer who detested my father's lazy, mocking air had refused to overlook his shortfall in attendance. Instead of applying himself to study, my father had spent more time reading storybooks and at cricket, basketball and swimming than in attending class. I heard that neither Lalita nor Kanti had reproached him and that the uncles had taken a lenient view of the matter. "Boys will be boys," they had said, closing ranks. My father had gone to Delhi to watch Sundarji march in India's first Republic Day parade in

1950 for which he had had to borrow a sweater for the cold from Sundarji, and his spare shoes, for he had no suitable ones of his own. He had had to stuff newspaper in the toes to fit in them. Sundarji, happy and uplifted after that memorable march, had said, "Sami, that was my first Republic Day parade," and they had laughed together when my father exulted, "It was everybody's first parade," and had a bit of a celebration.

Lalita had been delighted when my father was allotted a little house in Bapatla by the Hyderabad Agricultural Service. It had a garden with a lemon tree and a jasmine creeper. She had a home at last after twenty years of being on sufferance at Sita Sadan and felt restored in her own eyes after her long years of patient endurance to secure her children's future. I asked my father for details but all he said was, "She was very happy there. She cooked for me, kept house and taught the maid to read."

Lalita was dismayed when my father uprooted her from south India to live in rented barracks in Delhi, for Kanti had convinced him to sit for the Civil Services exam and he wrote it in Delhi and got into the revenue service, joining the Income-Tax department in 1951. He watched for the newspaper to be slid under the door every morning and one day it had the Civil Services list with his name and roll-number on it. Wildly elated, he dashed for confirmation to Parliament House where the list was posted and just after he found his name, there was a stir and a short, fair man had walked smiling through the crowd followed by the pleased murmur, "Punditji, Punditji." It was our first Prime Minister, Jawaharlal Nehru, and my father went back beaming to tell Lalita and Kanti.

Lalita had found refuge, then, I thought, first in Sarasvati, goddess of learning and art and at the very end with her son, from her wretched life as a south Indian brahmin widow. She had evolved from being a shy little bride and a tormented young widow to a self-taught reader who thought things through. She had become a free spirit who saw through false divisions. She had grown 'centred' and not repaid negativity with more negativity. Though reviled and repulsed as an unlucky woman, she had drawn people to her. She had made her life her witness.

That was worth having, I thought, though I felt very sorry that she had been passed like a parcel from her father to her husband to her brothers to her son, always having to adapt to their opinions and choices with no voice of her own. I wished very much that she was alive and in good health, living with me as the chieftan and goddess of my little household with no obligations or duties at all except light, pleasant ones that interested her; with the keys to the cupboards in her custody, a room of her own, her own bank account to draw upon as she chose and a car and driver to herself, free to go where she pleased, freely able to invite her friends over to tea, lunch and dinner, free to read as long as she liked in a comfortable chair, surrounded by flowers and plants, free to walk in Delhi's beautiful parks, free to hear all the music that she was of a mind to hear. But I was too late for Lalita.

I had a strong feeling though that had this wistful notion been possible—living with me, free of housekeeping and with no expectations except that she should enjoy herself—Lalita would not have stayed home reading novels, making the odd *rasam*, chanting the *Vishnu Sahasra Naamam* and being a textbook south Indian brahmin granny. I had a strong notion that she would have thrown herself into service for those with whom her deepest sympathies lay.

I could picture her quietly and happily volunteering at a cooperative for dalit women had they accepted her, sharing her skills and stories, cuddling the children and encouraging the girls to step out and seize life, helping them read Hindi, Urdu and English, sharing her books, sharing lunch, inviting them home for Dipavali and making Sita Sadan snacks for them, or if she was too frail to make them herself, telling me how to go about it and teaching them, too, if they liked our *murukku*, *thattai* and *thenguzhal*, our ribbon *pakoras* and our 'Madrasi mixture'.

What did 'freedom' mean I wondered, uncertain if there was any one answer to that fraught but necessary thought; surely it meant a genuine purpose beyond one's own small self; 'where never was heard a discouraging word' at home at least; and the small, simple but meaningful activities of life added up to peace and well-being, to a sense of keeping the human covenant? Why was that so difficult to achieve for a woman? Why had they kept Lalita dependent and shorn of dignity when she had been so eager to learn and earn, to pay for her own life?

She had gone on loving Srinivasa Sastri, I thought,

possibly because without that she would have felt worse, possibly because he really was nice in other ways, possibly because she was conditioned by Hindu myth to be the eternally faithful wife. Raghavaiyya had been a worshipper of the Devi and the tale of loyal, self-sacrificing divine princesses like Sati and Uma must have had its cultural impact.

I thought, too, of the verse in the south Indian brahmin wedding in the central rite of *kanyadaanam* when a father gives his daughter away to another man with King Janaka's Sanskrit words from the *Ramayana*, '*iyam Sita, mama suta*', 'this is Sita, my daughter'. Epic Sita had patiently borne every injustice, loving Ram to the end. But Sita was a goddess. Lalita was a frail human being of whom uncomplaining endurance was demanded by the millennia. And so, no doubt, she had loved Srinivasa, as behoved the *adarsh Bharatiya nari*, the ideal Indian woman, while he had done as he pleased.

I could not think well of Srinivasa Sastri knowing he had failed to protect his wife and children. I thought of small Kanti at six running lovingly and trustfully to him. He had let her fall, profaned her love and trust. I tried very hard to be non-judgemental but there was nowhere to hide from the fact that he had been 'weighed in the balance and found wanting', *mene mene tekel upharsin*.

I had that phrase from my father, who was fond of saying *'mene, mene'* in all kinds of situations. It was from the Book of Daniel in the Bible. These enigmatic words had appeared as 'the writing on the wall' at the feast of Belshazzar, the Babylonian king, after the sacred vessels from the Jewish temple at Jerusalem were profaned. Nobody could understand what it meant and the prophet Daniel had been called in. He had interpreted it as a judgement on the Babylonians and that night Belshazzar was killed and his city sacked. My father had shown me Rembrandt's painting of *Belshazzar's Feast* in one his art books and told me to read the story.

I put away Aunt Girija's letter about Srinivasa Sastri. Lalita remained an ache in my heart.

- *Five* -

Pro bono et vero, 'For the good and the true'. This is the motto of St Joseph's College, Trichnopoly or Tiruchirapalli, founded by the Jesuits in 1844 on vast acres donated by the then Nawab of Arcot. It is where my mother's father, Dr S.V. Ganapati, graduated from in 1921 in Chemistry, with Physics as his second subject. When not sniffing at nasty odours or peering at micro-organisms in the lab, which he was to do all his life as a biochemist, 'Thatha', my grandfather, was out on the football field with his Christian, Muslim and Anglo-Indian friends. Few brahmin boys of his time played football, they preferred cricket, which was considered more 'stylish' and had no body contact. My grandfather, who loved the game, did not miss their company. His brahminical tuft and sacred thread had come off early in school and he wore western clothes. He may even have said "Bugger off," to any brahmin boy who had the nerve

to comment, a term picked up from his football gang in Trichy which slipped out sometimes in later life.

Thatha was born on 1 January 1900, as the second son of extremely orthodox brahmin parents in Srinivasanallur village on the north bank of the Kaveri, in Trichy district deep in the old Chola country. His father was a priest and not a bit rich. Srinivasanallur was close to the historical town of Musiri, derived from 'Muskundapuri', named after the mythological

St Joseph's College, Trichy, in the 1920s

king Muskunda in the second century Tamil epics *Silappadikaram* and *Manimekhalai*. Srinivasanallur village lay in a green and pleasant land called Mahendramangalam in ancient days, an agrarian belt along the Kaveri that was rich in rice, sugarcane, fruit and vegetables. Fine reed mats made of *korai* grass were a local specialty. Indifferent to who ruled the land, life went dreaming by as it had for centuries at the Srinivasanallur *agraharam* or brahmin quarter, its calendar highlights being the festivals at the local temple whose patron had been a ninth century Chola king.

But Thatha's father, Venkataramana Iyer, must have had a wake-up call at some point for he moved to Trichy city about fifty km away for the education of his sons. I do not know the details of Thatha's elder brother's life for we almost never met except the one time on a visit to Madras. I have only a dim memory of his son, my uncle Sitaraman, and his family, an impression of affectionate people who fed us very good traditional food. We lost touch with them and a great many other people after my mother's death. But I do know that my grandfather was sent to the Hindu Secondary School in Trichy. The best college education in the region was to be had at St

Jesuits at St Joseph's College in my grandfather's day.

Joseph's and there he was next despatched. Although slightly older than his classmates because of his late start at school, he had, he said, the time of his life. The Jesuits were brilliant teachers and the college prided itself on its history and made sure to give its students every modern scientific tool and gadget available in the British Empire.

Thatha's father, for all his slender means and rigid personal orthodoxy, may have worked it out with *Kaveri karai* 'smarts', for people from 'the banks of the Kaveri' were said to be sharp-witted. His elder son would stay orthodox to satisfy custom, which he was apparently glad to do. The younger son was set free to be as modern as he pleased. I wonder if his birthday had something to do with it. Perhaps Thatha's father had the notion that since his younger son was born on the first day of the new century he should be given to the new age, and struck off his gyves. I do not know if Thatha had to earn his tuition grinding *idli* batter in the big granite querns of the College kitchens as I heard poor brahmin boys did those days to pay their way. Perhaps not, given that almost all his free time went to football.

Thatha's next move was to head north to Madras to look for work. He showed up in 1922 at the office of Major C. Cunningham, IMS, the Indian Medical Service, at the King Institute, Guindy, and was appointed as the first ever water analyst of the Waterworks of the Madras Municipal Corporation. It is strange to think that while my father's father was out lotus-eating at the race course in Guindy my mother's father was being rigorously trained by Cunningham in the methods of water and sewage analysis. After a year, Thatha was given independent charge of the new laboratory created by the municipal corporation.

This was radical work for the son of an orthodox brahmin and showed how much the new scientific temper of the age could change those who were receptive to it. No lawyer's robe for Thatha, but a lab coat and practical problems affecting public health to work on. Not that he had an opinion on others, it was *loko bhinna ruchi*, or 'tastes differ', as the Sanskrit saying had it. To instil this open attitude, Thatha had me learn and recite *The Mountain and the Squirrel* by Emerson, it was a family favourite: "*Talents differ; all is well and wisely put; If I cannot carry forests on my back, Neither can you crack a nut.*" As long as he could do the work he did, why, so might all others with his best goodwill. His life was his witness. His colleagues were scientists, municipal workers, sweepers, scavengers, fisherfolk, boatmen and the rural poor; down-to-earth people with songs and stories as eloquent as that of the uptown aesthetes but unrecognised. What the priests did symbolically, Thatha and his colleagues did literally, which was to purify the waters.

The Madras Waterworks at Kilpauk had been opened by Lord Pentland in 1913. Thereafter, its fourteen slow sand filters began to emit hydrogen sulphide, which had the worst smell on earth. In effect, the filtered water supply of Madras smelt terrible. This was not because of sewage leaks into the clean water. There was a mystery bug inside the filters and nobody knew what it was. An Expert Committee chose the method of conducting lots of experiments on lots of small sample filters to see which one would yield a clue. My grandfather cut to the chase with direct research, working without a guide. It turned out to be a bacterium that reduced the sulphates in the water, resulting in the smell.

This awful problem was finally solved after years of research and my grandfather submitted his investigations as a thesis for his M.Sc. which he was awarded by Madras University followed by the Sir William Wedderburn Prize.

Wedderburn, 1838-1918, had been a Scottish civil servant in India. He had proposed the setting up of agricultural cooperative banks to give the Indian farmer credit at reasonable rates so as to escape the moneylenders. But his proposal was blocked by the India

Office and, unable to find support for his reforms, he had retired to help found the Indian National Congress and support local self-government. So this was a meaningful prize for practical public service.

Thatha next submitted a monograph to Madras University on the limnology of the Red Hills Reservoir that was the source of raw water to Madras. Limnology was the study of inland waters, an evolving environmental science those days and this fetched him the Maharaja of Travancore-Curzon Prize.

Just as he had balanced classroom hours with football at St Joseph's, Thatha divided his work between the laboratory and the field. He loved wandering through remote rural reaches, water-sample bottles in a canvas rucksack, notebook and dipper to hand, exploring the lakes, reservoirs, rivers and *aeri,* the ponds of the Madras Presidency. He was a prowling 'bug man' and an admirer of the Danish naturalist Johann Gerhard Koenig, 1728-1785, a surgeon and a botanist trained by the great Carl Linnaeus. Koenig had come out to India to the Dutch settlement of Tranquebar. Short of funds, he had worked as a naturalist for the Nawab of Arcot in 1774 before joining the British East India Company, which had later sent him to Siam. Koenig was considered the first modern botanist in India, which had its own ancient authorities on plants. In the Tamil country, these were identified by Sangam poetry as typical of each of the *Ai Vagai* or 'Five Terrains', from the ocean to the hills, while ancient Siddha and Ayurveda plant knowledge had been practiced for millennia. Combining the exploration of his region with western scientific methods, Thatha began to publish papers on his studies in Indian and foreign scientific journals. He liked and lived the robust maxim

Two worlds melded—the Rock Fort temple at Trichy with St Joseph's College in the foreground.

of the old Roman poet Juvenal that came with a colonial education, *mens sana in corpore sano*, 'a sound mind in a sound body'.

His next call to service was as shockingly unorthodox as the first. The Directorate of Fisheries of the Madras Government had newly expanded its department. Thatha was borrowed on deputation from the Waterworks as the Fisheries hydrologist. In his six years on the job, 1945 to 1951, Thatha published many scientific papers, on matters like 'industrial pollution of manmade lakes', 'aquatic manuring', 'bionomics of the Indian major carp', 'acclimatisation of salt water fish seed to fresh water', 'large-scale fish mortality in ponds', 'spawning of fish in rivers' and 'fish fly transport'. I owe these details to a biographical sketch of Thatha written in 1980 by a fellow-scientist, Dr D.K. Belsare, for the Dutch scientific journal *Hydrobiologia*.

By the early 1950s Thatha had nearly fifty papers to his credit, the slow, steady work of years, which he submitted as a doctoral thesis called 'Studies on the inland waters and waste waters of Madras State', the first such, for which he was awarded his D.Sc by Madras University in 1956 as well as the Andhra University

Medal. I don't know whether the university sent the state government a copy of this study or other such studies for the reference of its urban planners. It seems unlikely that the urban planners of free India considered these matters in the rush of 'development' that befell Madras not very long after Independence.

Meanwhile, the Indian capital's filtered water supply urgently needed a quality control mission. Thatha had just retired from the Madras Government Waterworks, and the Municipal Corporation of Delhi rushed him north. The Delhi Joint Water and Sewage Board asked him to be their Chief Water Analyst for four years. Thatha was asked by Madras University, while in Delhi, to come back to deliver a series of six lectures on waste water management under the Maharaja of Travancore-Curzon Endowment to engineering students. He was wanted next as the water adviser on Delhi's Environment Board and after that it was the Gujarat government that sent for him, at Ahmedabad and Baroda. Thatha worked for some time in Ahmedabad and came to roost in the Department of Biochemistry, MS University, Baroda, living in its staff quarters, the Adhyapak Kutir, to which I was a frequent visitor in childhood. This university was founded by the enlightened Maratha ruler of Baroda state, Maharaja Sayaji Rao Gaekwad III and was privately owned and funded. The Biochemistry department attracted many independent minds, including the Tambrahm scientists Rajalakshmi Ramakrishnan and her husband C.V. Ramakrishnan, who was the head of the department for many years. Their son, Venkitaraman Ramakrishnan, born in Chidambaram, became a structural biologist who went to England and America, shared the Nobel Prize for Chemistry in 2009 and became the President of the Royal Society in 2015. Thatha, from what I gathered in later years, greatly enjoyed himself in the independent atmosphere of MS University.

After my mother's sudden death in 1973, Thatha moved to Bhopal to stay with his youngest daughter, my aunt Malati, whose engineer husband worked there. My aunt's husband left Bhopal after some years to become a farmer in Kodaikanal where he had land. Kodaikanal was a lovely town in the Palani Hills, Tamil Nadu, set up by the British in 1845 as a health resort with a strong American missionary presence. The concept of organic food or health food had begun to get popular in the west and my aunt, a keen gardener and champion of natural food, opened an avant-garde shop in Kodi called 'The Eco-Nut' where she sold organic food, Siddha and Ayurveda products and home-made trail-mix, muesli, bread and muffins. She later opened a branch in Besant Nagar, Madras. My grandfather, I felt sure, would have thoroughly approved of such work.

During his years in Bhopal, Thatha's principal mission in life was to assist young scientists at Bhopal University who were handicapped by poor English. He helped them write or polish their theses, also encouraging other shy, but bright, sincere young people find their feet on the slippery slope of scientific institutions. The Madhya Pradesh Government made Thatha a consultant on their rivers and lakes. Later, he also did the index for my father's doctoral thesis on tax law, spending a whole summer on the task.

UNESCO invited Thatha through the 1960s and 1970s to seminars and conferences and as the head of a steering committee of the International Biological Programme while foreign governments invited him to be the rapporteur on scientific gatherings. He travelled to France, England and Wales, Poland, Bulgaria, the old GDR, Israel and Malaysia. He got me a smart pencil-cum-compass box from Paris that my mother refused to let me show off at school in Bombay and a fine book of maps of the Jewish holy land from Jerusalem. He was not the sort to buy cheese and chocolate but had I asked for a particular book, I would have got it.

His birthday presents to me were the novels of Walter Scott and Alexandre Dumas, *The Count of Monte Cristo* being a favourite. My mother laughed when she saw that and said Thatha was gifting me all her favourites. I remember her saying dreamily, *"The burning sun of Syria had not yet reached its zenith..."* from *The Talisman* by Sir Walter Scott. Years later when I chanced to be in Marseilles, I took the boat out to circle the Chateau d'If where Dumas's hero had been imprisoned. Thanks to my mother and Thatha, every corner of Europe and the UK that I went to had some story for me and so had Damascus where I made sure to salute 'Saladin' and admire his magnificent statue on horseback.

My grandfather had a tiny 'bug' named after him, the chydorid *Indialona ganapati*, which had proved to be a new discovery, a separate genus. Finding a new type of 'sublittoral plankton' in the waters of the Ajwa Reservoir, Ahmedabad, in 1966, and unable to identify it himself, he had mailed off water samples to the famous Russian hydrobiologist Petkovski at Moscow. Thatha was taken aback when several international researchers asked him about it some months later at a science conference abroad. Petkovski had named it after Thatha, written a scientific paper assigning it to a new genus and absent-mindedly forgotten to tell him. After Thatha's death in 1982, Tokyo University published a commemorative volume of papers on limnology in his honour. It seems my aunts discovered a number of medals, awards and honours that he had put away in his Godrej *almirah* and never mentioned.

Thatha's work was not glamorous, it was hardcore applied science. It was the difference between life and death for 'cities, and thrones and powers'. I think he would have identified with dalit writer-academic Professor Gopal Guru's statement that "Indian social science represents a pernicious divide between theoretical Brahmins and empirical Shudras." Thatha did field work and if he found something interesting, he documented it. It seems he was an atheist although he did not denounce the believing, it was *loko bhinna ruchi* in this, too. He liked my school motto 'Work is Worship'

at Hill Grange High School on Pedder Road and related more to Zarathushtra's ancient credo that "working hands are better than praying hands" than to warring creeds and their dogmas and rituals.

Consequently, his three daughters had hands-on, down-to-earth skills besides being taught to cultivate their minds. Tall, slim and elegantly turned out, my mother's elder sister Rajalakshmi, 'Rajam Periamma' to me, had taken the Madras University gold medal in Sanskrit from Queen Mary's College. When she married an engineer, K.R. Srinivasan, and went off to the iron and steel mills town of Burnpur in the 'Great Ruhr' of West Bengal, she kept a good table and a nice home. Her dress-making was exquisite and I happily wore her daughter Amala's hand-me-down frocks through childhood and looked forward to the big tin of home-made 'California rock cookies' that she sent us at Dipavali.

Thatha had been urged to marry after

he found a job. But he was definite that not only did his bride have to slim and fair, no let-up there for the centuries went too deep, but also that she had to be properly educated. This was not an easy package to deliver in the 1920s.

His parents cast about and discovered that a "horse-riding brahmin in the Indian Police Service", not so usual those days in the Madras Presidency, had a pink, pretty daughter who had been sent to school wherever he had been posted. Her sister was married to a man whose brother had been sent to medical college in England and was to write FRCS, Fellow of the Royal College of Surgeons, after his name. Ponnammal loved to read English books and was something of a language fiend. She preferred Tamil to Sanskrit, being steeped in Tamil lore, and was keen to learn Hindi. She adored music and was trained to cook and keep house. She was used to being the only girl in school. Her desk and chair were placed in front at a right angle to the teacher's desk. The rest of the class, all boys, was arranged as usual, facing the teacher's desk and the blackboard behind it. She was paralysed with fright at first but was expected to be brave as a policeman's daughter and managed to keep her composure.

Above:
Rajam Periamma and Srinivasan Periappa, left, with my parents.

Below:
Calcutta kids—with my cousin Sriram and his sister Amala (right).

The boys recognised *adakkam* when they saw it and did not trouble Ponni though it was hard, no doubt, for a pretty girl to escape being stared at. I remember a startling thing she told me when I was about nine or ten. "Men," she said, "will stare at a stick with a sari wrapped around it if you take one down the street. You be careful of men." She also instilled old-fashioned 'maidenly reserve' in me with Tamil sayings like, *'Penn siricha podhum, pogai-elai viricha podhum.'* 'A girl's reputation is gone if she smiles, a tobacco-leaf will not curl back once it opens.'

Ponni and Thatha

I was to hear many scornful remarks in later years about "repressed Tambrahm women" but I don't think the ones I knew were repressed, they were merely private. They routinely taught their female young to be careful in public, which still seems a sensible idea. For instance, in my otherwise curiously lax little whiskey-*sambar* world, my father did not raise hell in my late teens if I smoked a cigarette and had a drink, the key, he said, being moderation. And, "You can do anything you like within reason," my mother had said, "if you speak politely." This life code bought me considerable freedom later when I had to fend for myself amid the 'Taliban Lite'. Old-fashioned politeness, I found, was indeed the key to India; it was the armour, bridge and escape route in our old society. It was in music that a nice Tambrahm girl was expected to let herself go without holding back, which we would perhaps now call 'sublimation'.

My mother's people never talked about their family but just got on with life, so I never heard tales about my great-grandfather in the *polis*. But knowing my weakness for a *kathai* or story, Ponni told me European fairy tales, the edited myths of Greece, Rome and Egypt, Indian folktales of tricksters and heroes and many stories from

The Arabian Nights. I liked Sindbad the Sailor best, and the brothers Nuruddin and Badruddin whose special family recipe for a sweet reunited them after many mishaps.

"Paati, *kathai*," I begged every day and was never disappointed. Strangely, she never told me tales from the two Hindu epics. Indian children's periodicals like *Chandamama* and mytho-comics like *Amar Chitra Katha* showed up at home merely as more stories, *Vikram and the Vetaal* being the most interesting.

This extraordinary omission was explained when I overheard my mother and grandmother talking in our flat on Pedder Road in Bombay; you couldn't help it sometimes in a flat even if you were not the type to creep about.

My mother said, "I don't want her mental growth stunted. Some of those stories simply won't do," and my granny said, "I only told her about the squirrel at Setu and how it got its stripes."

"So why was she crying?"

"I had to tell her why they built the bridge and she cried about Sita being alone and frightened like Lalita Paati."

"We'd better go to the zoo again," said my mother. "Let her observe the animals and you can say it was just a nice little story, nothing to do with real life."

This time I did not run in to confess, not only because I wanted to think it over but also because I did not want to lose face with my granny when my mother scolded.

Finally, I braced myself to ask my mother. "You had no business to stand around listening," glared my mother, "I hate to think you're an eavesdropper." "I didn't mean to," I pleaded. "But now that I've heard it, please tell me what you meant?"

My mother suddenly drew me close. "I want you to be free in your mind, be free to be happy. Don't make yourself unhappy; don't let others make you unhappy. There is so much to be happy about. Count your blessings. Always count your blessings," she said. I hugged her back, not really understanding it then.

She must have discussed it with my father, who sat me down to learn *An die Freude* in German, Schiller's *Ode to Joy,* with only a few outbreaks of impatience since he found it boring to teach children. His attempt to tutor me in Math had been a disaster and he had slapped me for being stupid, which had sent me weeping to my mother who had patted my head, told me to wash my face and gone to speak to him, shutting the door behind her. But this was fun and I was all attention and interest. It had to be written down, the German had to be explained word by word along with the *umlaut*; the German and its English translation had to be copied neatly and finally my father, who could really sing well, taught me to sing it until I 'got it pat'. Such labour-intensive diversionary tactics by my mother, for it was her idea, helped as she knew they would, to deracinate me as we would now say. I had no defence against songs and stories, which is why she wanted to protect me from the doomed epic heroines for as long as she could or at least build a strong mental buffer first.

Since inhabiting multiple realities is the ultimate Indian mental rope trick, none of this had anything to do with Bharata Natyam, which was intensely Hindu epic-based. Thatha had lived in Egmore, when my mother was a little girl, out in the Great Choultry Plain inland from Fort St George, which had first been settled by the English with garden houses. However much a modern man of science, he was nevertheless from the *Kaveri karai*, a region steeped in Carnatic music. He was also a sturdy supporter of the freedom movement and believed in the ongoing Indian cultural renaissance that made twentieth-century life so interesting in the Madras Presidency.

Just as Srinivasa Sastri was part of the Suguna Vilasa Sabha, Thatha became a member of the Indian Fine Arts Society that promoted traditional Indian music and dance. The 'anti-Nautch' campaign had felled an entire sub-culture of Hindu temple dance and the 'fallen' *devadasis* or temple dancers were in hiding from society. Champions like E. Krishna Iyer, incidentally a member of the Suguna Vilasa Sabha, took up the cause of *sadir*, the dances of the *devadasis*. Two power centres of *sadir* developed, which became known as 'Bharata Natyam', the dance of India, in that nationalist phase. One, in Mylapore in the heart of town, was ruled by the traditional artiste Balasaraswathi; the second, on the outskirts of south Madras at Adyar, was the Kalakshetra dance school founded by the beautiful south Indian brahmin Rukmini Devi Arundale, who had already scandalised society by marrying an Englishman and was spurred to discover dance forms at home by none other than Anna Pavlova, met on board a ship to Australia.

Rukmini Devi had brought Pandanallur Meenakshi Sundaram Pillai to Kalakshetra from the Kaveri Delta.

He was a teacher of *sadir* from a famous lineage of gurus and his nephew Chokkalingam Pillai began to teach the dance independently in Egmore. Thatha asked his daughters if they wished to learn. This was a greatly daring thing to do those days, someone from a non-artiste family learning the dance of the *devadasis*. But Rukmini Devi had shown the way; and Thatha, a friend of E. Krishna Iyer (I found a file of his letters to Thatha) was all for it. My mother, the middle daughter, wanted to learn *sadir* for she loved dancing at school events to the Hindi *bhajans* or devotional songs that were the vogue in Madras. Ponni, who had passed exams in Hindi and loved the language, had chosen songs for her like *Krishna Kanhaiya bansiwala* and Shanta Apte's *Kanha sab ko mohe mangal roop tumhara* from the Hindi film *Gopal Krishna*. This film, produced by Sheikh Fatehlal Yasin and Vishnupant Damle of the pioneering Prabhat Studios, Bombay, had thrilled Madras in 1938 when my mother was nine.

After several interviews, Thatha chose Rafael, a sober, reliable rickshaw man, to take my mother to Chokkalingam Pillai's dance class every morning at six am. He paid for her classes and paid for her dance debut

Janiki in a typical *Mohiniattam* pose.

Ram Gopal and Chandrabhaga Devi in typical *Bharata Natya* poses. Note the clean lines of their arms.

Srimathi Balasaraswathi.

Krishna Rao and Chandrabhaga Devi —two fine teachers of *Bharata Natya.*

Above: Kumari Kausalya, an outstanding dancer of the Pandanallur style of *Bharata Natya.*
Below: Rukmini Devi of Adyar.

Photographs of Balasaraswati, Rukmini Devi and Kausalya in "The Other Mind: A Study of Dance in South India" by Beryl de Zoete, 1953.

with its expenses of costumes and accompanists' fees while supporting his own family and that of a relative who was going through hard times, also contributing to his elderly parents' upkeep. My grandmother's managerial skills were well-tested.

When we lived in Calcutta, my mother's household arrangements as a working woman would tumble down if Mahua Sinha, my day-minder, had to take off to attend to her own family duties. However, my mother was keen that I should be left in the care of an educated lady in my early years and accommodated Mahua's plans. Just before Mahua's long leaves, my mother would buy plane tickets with her own salary to Ahmedabad or Baroda, going from one end of India to the other to drop me off at Thatha's on a Saturday, flying back to Calcutta on Sunday so that she could go back to office on Monday. As the first lady officer in her service, she evidently went to great lengths to set an example and ensure that nobody could say she was taking advantage at work of being a woman. This was the pattern during our five years in Calcutta until we

Kausalya at sixteen dressed up by Ponni in a davani or 'half-sari'.

were transferred to Bombay. It was easier then, for Ponni Paati to take the train from Baroda to Bombay to see my mother through any number of crises and official tours away.

Air-freighting me across the width of India from West Bengal to Gujarat solved my mother's problem in those early years but drove my Thatha mad because I did irritating things like repeatedly throwing my doll out and setting up a wail for it. Thatha would have to fetch it every time to restore peace and one day he threatened to throw me out if I did that again. My grandmother clucked in protest but it worked on the *piriki*. They took me to Gir Forest to see the lions and I liked it so much that I wanted us to get down from the Jeep. Thatha told my mother that he had been sorely tempted to leave me behind as lion-food for being such a nuisance. He would get cross if I troubled her and snap, "Leave my daughter alone!" My days with Thatha-Paati are a happy blur of being the centre of attention, with both growls and hugs, of story after story and bowls of nicely cold bits of guava, *chikoo* or mango.

Thatha's house was also where I discovered *farsaan*, the extraordinary range of Gujarati savoury snacks. The *chivda* was the best thing I'd eaten in my greedy little life and huge five-kilo tins would be sent to us from Gujarat at Dipavali, "to feed your beast," said my grandfather's card. With Thatha, Ponni and Kausalya gone for decades now, it is Gujarati *chivda*, not south Indian food, which powerfully brings back my *nanihal* or 'mother's mother's house' as the fond Hindi term goes.

My grandfather wrote me several letters after my mother died and so did Ponni. Especially, Thatha warned me that my enthusiasms were "like bottled soda, going flat after the first rush of bubbles." But I discovered that Kausalya had taken them away with her. We were in Kanti's house for the first three years after my mother's death and their bond with my father, who became a recluse overnight, rapidly loosened. Thatha faded from my life after the summer that he came to stay with us in Delhi to prepare the index for my father's thesis; it must have been his last labour of love for his dead daughter.

He asked me on that visit, too, to recite poetry and I fetched my book to read *Autumn Leaves* by Auden. The menace in it had given me nightmares in school until Kanti disclosed that she had been taken to tea with Auden by a friend in Oxford. She had never seen

so many wrinkles on a face, she said, and had been as fascinated looking as listening. The nightmares stopped and it was an act of courage restored to read it to Thatha. He liked it and asked next for Thomas Gray's *Elegy Written in a Country Churchyard*. I was going through a phase of disdaining the eighteenth century and Victorian poets and said, "*Chhee*, not that." He said, "Well then, *mochakottai*," which was Ponni's name for me, meaning 'little lima bean' in Tamil, and went away. I wish I had had the grace to recite it when he asked.

My Paati, such a tremendous presence when Kausalya was alive, faded away, too. My grandparents seemed half-dead themselves after they lost her. I count it a blessing that I had them through childhood and my brother and sister, who were unable to relate to them, stared to hear it. Thatha would probably have snorted, "Get on with your work, lazy buggers."

Thatha at seventy-plus.

- Six -

I cannot begin to imagine how my aunt Kanti grew up without going insane. Her mother Lalita had a full, happy life before Hindu widowhood robbed her of dignity. I had beautiful memories of my mother to both torment and sustain me and if I did not do better academically after her death or make wiser choices it was my fault for not being made of sterner stuff. But Kanti's last memory of being cuddled at home was at age six when she ran to be swung up in her father's arms. After Srinivasa Sastri's death Lalita, only twenty-six, was so lost in grief for her husband and for her three dead children, that she did not realise how traumatised her two remaining children were.

My father remembers being told by older cousins that they had seen his father being taken away tied to a pole, to be burnt. He was just over two years old and wept in terror, running a high temperature for days. Lalita was so distraught that she barely noticed when my father caught small-pox, the dreaded 'Amman', called 'Mata' in the north. Luckily he recovered after a long illness. But his appearance was dramatically changed. From being a pink, plump toddler he had turned into a pock-marked stick, the marks taking several years to fade. My father's big cousin, Ramamurthi, told me a story about it in the late 1970s. Ramamurthi read Political Science in Geneva and became Dr. C.V.L. Narayana, one of the young men in Krishna Menon's London Majlis, and a staunch Congress worker when he came back to live in Chittoor. He was a brahmin with a dalit constituency and the local upper caste landlords detested him. He never married and his parents moved to Bangalore to live with his younger brother, my father's favourite cousin, C.V. Chandrasekhar, 'Sekhar Periappa' to us. Ramamurthi was found murdered in their family home 'Gowri Kumar' in Chittoor in the 1990s, evidently having put up a big fight, for the walls were covered in blood and the furniture knocked all over the place, said the cousins. They never found out who killed him. 'Ramutthi' as his cousins called him had been away in college when Lalita, newly widowed, went back to Chittoor. He came home to

Gowri Kumar on a visit late in 1930 and went calling on Sita Sadan, which was close by. He did not recognise my father who was playing between the flower beds in the courtyard and sternly shooed him out, thinking he was a little intruder from the street. A passing aunt reproached him, "That's Lalita's son, why are you chasing him out?" "That can't be 'Sami'," he said, sitting down in shock.

After that bad start, my father had a free, happy childhood and teenage. Being a boy, he could play all day and roam about without restraint. He explored the garden, the *gadikhana*, the cowshed, the street, the market and the neighbour's houses and flew kites from all the rooftops he could reach. Being a well-favoured little boy he was a sort of universal pet and some aunt or neighbour lady was always calling him in to taste something special made that day. He played cricket with his many male cousins, climbed trees, sent wooden tops spinning, cracked marbles, played carrom, swung from anything that could be swung from, hit anything that could be hit, jumped over anything that could be jumped over, ran up and down stairs and corridors, walked precariously along roof edges and terrace ledges for dares

Lalita's sister Manju and her husband, the benign deities of 'Gowri Kumar'.

and became a strong swimmer. He went camping as a Boy Scout and then as a cadet in the UTC or University Training Corps, precursor of the military-oriented NCC, the National Cadet Corps. He slept in tents, climbed, hiked, drilled, played every game he could play, especially basket-ball, for he had inherited the long Tandalam bones and grew to be six feet tall.

When he was a little boy, he liked to run barefoot behind the horse-drawn carriage of his uncle, Ramamurthi's father, who was a High Court vakil in Chittoor. This uncle was especially kind and caring to my father, Lalita and Kanti, buying them new clothes at Dipavali to make up for the truly awful hand-me-downs that came their way at Sita Sadan where Tripurasundari ruled.

Uncle Sekhar's bride, Leela, who lit up 'Gowri Kumar' in later years with her gentle, pretty ways, remembered it well, coming from a liberal family herself. Her own grandfather was a Rao Bahadur who had once worked as the Dewan of Bharatpur state far away in the deeply conservative north. He had made sure to find liberal, service-minded families to ally his clan with, refusing to consider those rich, young Tambrahm men who were

Aunt Leela's grandfather in court dress as Dewan.

disinclined to study and work. The north Indian rulers often sent for administrators from the south those days, said Aunt Leela, to help them negotiate with the British whom south Indians had known for so much longer. But the bowing and scraping of an old-fashioned durbar usually proved too much for English-educated south Indian brahmin men who were used to more modern ways and grew wary of such appointments unless the ruler was westernised and modern, too, and qualified as 'enlightened' in his intentions towards his subjects. Gowri Kumar, I realised, had been an occasional haven of sorts to Lalita and Kanti from the rigours of Sita Sadan.

There were two vast libraries to browse in at will, at Sita Sadan and at Gowri Kumar, where Manjubhashini, Lalita's elder sister, was as good-natured as her husband. My father devoured everything that came to hand including copies of *Punch* and *The Spectator* from England. His favorite books were *The Adventures of Peregrine Pickle* by Tobias Smollet and thereby, *The Pickwick Papers*. He was so taken with Dickens that he even said, "Barkis is willin'" when it was proposed years later that he should marry Kausalya. I don't think my mother, the superstar, who knew her nineteenth century English novels as well as he did, was perfectly pleased being cast as 'Peggoty' but she maintained that she was "absolutely thrilled" to find him so tall and handsome.

My father "fed on honey-dew and drank the milk of Paradise" he said, curled up with a storybook or out playing in Chittoor. The men of the house were fed first and my father sat in the same row as the uncles and male cousins while the women and girls ran to and fro to serve them coffee or milk when they woke up, and the big morning meal before they went to work or school. When they came home in the afternoon around three or four pm, they sat down again to tiffin, which was a choice of snacks—*upma, vadai, dosai* or *adai*, and fruit and sweets. A fresh batch of batter would be made every three days and the practice was to make *idlis* the first day when the batter was at its most fresh and fluffy, *dosais* on the second day and *uthappam* the third day, when it was slightly fermented. This is the batter-drill that I remember, too, from Ponni's and Kausalya's kitchens. The evening meal was light, like the tiffin, and as always the men and boys were the first to eat and could ask for as much as they wanted. Lalita and Kanti ate last of all in the family.

In the hot weather, the servants and girls squeezed orange juice or pomegranate juice for the boys or made mango milkshakes and salted buttermilk. They made 'fruit ice' or sorbets of *chikoo*, grapes, plum, pineapple, custard apple, mango or very ripe guavas, carefully seeded. Big baskets of fruit and vegetables would come down from the hills and my father remembers an interesting *sambar* with Brussels sprouts.

The kitchens at Sita Sadan and Gowri Kumar were run like little factories for the snack tins could never be allowed to empty and there was an endless round of festivals, each with its prescribed ritual or seasonal food. Besides all this, there were little wafers called *vadaam* to be made and little discs of *poppadum* and big discs of *appalam*. There were chips to fry every week of potato, banana and jackfruit, and seasonal pickles to put up in great china jars, at least three kinds of lemon pickle and five kinds of mango, said my grand-aunts.

The lead-up to Dipavali was intense in these kitchens with the making of salted snacks like *murukku, thattai, sheedai, thenkuzhal* and '*ribbon pakora*' and sweets like *jaangiri, padusha, laddoos* speckled with cashewnuts, raisins and camphor, almond *halva* and almond *barfi*, coconut *barfi* and *rava laddoo*. A rare treat was *paluda* or *kulfi-faluda* also known by its charming name in faraway Madurai as *jil-jil jigar thanda* or cold cooler.

My father's right to school fees, school books, shoes, uniforms and sports was not questioned although he was a charity child, his every expense, including the occasional doctor's bill paid for by his mother's brothers. My father was a boy who would one day be a man. This was his entitlement. He brought home a prize now and then for sports or essay-writing. He loved singing and acting and even took a prize, to his great astonishment, at the Chittoor Board High School, for singing a funny little Tamil song he had made up as one of two bumbling policemen come to arrest the thief in *The Bishop's Candlesticks*. Almost anything he did was considered amusing or creditable.

My father once wondered what the world would look like upside down and to test this novel notion, tried to walk down the venerable stairs of Sita Sadan on his hands. Lalita's eldest brother bumped into him and caught the acrobat by his ankles. This uncle had a pet name for my father, 'Pauranikar', meaning 'the Story-teller' as at courtyards and temples. My father read so much that he was never short of a story to tell at the dullest gathering and this was praised as a mark of cleverness. He picked up songs as soon as he heard them and should have begun Carnatic music lessons right away but this is where the uncles balked. No music lessons for my father, it was an "unnecessary" expense. Years later, it was my mother who found my father a music teacher. It was her present to him on their first wedding anniversary, she paid for the lessons.

Lalita was more upset by this than by several other things though of course she could not say so since she was doomed forever to be grateful. She taught my father whatever she had learned herself from Chittoor Subrahmanya Pillai as a very young girl in that very house. But my father's thirst for music only grew and Lalita tried to find a solution. The local temple had a fine *nagaswaram* pipe player and the *odhuvar*, the ritual singer, would walk around the temple courtyard at set times every day with the temple orchestra of pipes and drums, singing and playing in the classical *ragas*. My granny told my father to go hear the *ragas* played at the temple, ask for their names and try to sing them. My father took along a little pocket diary, passed on by a big cousin, for his music jottings.

I went to at least thirty Carnatic concerts with my father in Delhi between my eighteenth and twentieth birthdays, some at Vigyan Bhavan and Mavlankar Hall. They were also held at the auditorium of the Sardar Patel Vidyalaya, a school down the lane from where we lived. It was a time of fragile peace between us and we heard many Carnatic singers and musicians in their prime. My father would always pull out a tiny diary and turn over its pages, closely written over with notes, to check the provenance of the songs. I did not hear of his early lack of music lessons until I was older, which is when I realised that the diary habit went back to his childhood as a *chiffonier*, a rag-picker of music at the temple.

The uncles did not think it necessary to educate Kanti. But my granny insisted when Kanti was eight that she should be sent to school so that she could teach and earn her living one day. The uncles said she would have to be married but nobody suitable would marry a fatherless girl who could not be married "properly" and they would be obliged to find Kanti some poor man who would be willing to take a well-born girl for free. They said it was enough if she could read and do household accounts. Tripurasundari said nobody would want to marry Kanti because she was "dark" and not "beautiful" like her mother and aunts. She was vehemently opposed to Kanti's education, more than her sons.

Ringed by dragons, Lalita quietly stood her ground although she must have been terrified inside and politely asked them not only to send Kanti to school but also let her have music lessons. This gave the uncles a ladder to climb down without losing face. They said Kanti could either go to school or have music lessons. So my granny said that she wanted her daughter to be educated. But the uncles added a caveat to pacify their angry mother. They said Kanti had to get the highest marks in class each year if she wanted to go to the next one.

There was nowhere in all of Sita Sadan that Kanti could be private in or study peacefully and she was frequently interrupted by her grandmother for a new chore. Tripurasundari, a sore loser, never stopped saying how dark, ugly and poor Kanti was and that she was destined to be a burden on earth, of no use to anybody with her lack of looks, skills and dower. I don't think Kanti always managed to be the first in class but she pushed herself hard to study so that she never slid below the top five. If Lalita caught Kanti reading a frivolous storybook, she beat her with her *visiri kattai*, the wooden handle of her stout palmetto fan. Lalita had bought Kanti's school fees with her pride and did not mean to have her daughter squander her luck. The pressure to escape indignity through study ruled Kanti's life from the age of eight, from 1931. Lalita and Kanti earned their keep and my father's by doing a heavy share of the household chores at Sita Sadan. The sisters-in-law would sometimes call their own daughters in to eat something special while Kanti was given a handful of rice flakes like Sudama in reverse. Lalita never said a word or showed she was discomfited or downcast and Kanti said implacably later, "I loathe self-pity." They were like epic princesses in their unassailable dignity and kept up a cheerful front for the most part although it must have been hard sometimes.

Being a girl, Kanti was not allowed out of the house, not even to look out at the street from the front door or to visit an aunt or cousin in the neighbourhood unless suitably escorted. She could not even go to the temple unless with my granny or an aunt. The market was too exotic and dangerous a possibility to be considered. Kanti was told from when she was barely seven or eight to behave like a woman and was not allowed to run, skip, play hopscotch or play with dolls. She tried when she was about ten to make herself a cloth doll with left-over bits from her cousins' party clothes but was scolded so badly by her grandmother that she threw it away in fright. Lalita was so humiliated by this that she gave Kanti a severe beating with the *kattai,* dragging her into the bathroom, locking the door behind her and thrashing Kanti hard. She brought along a cup of warm herbal oil later to anoint Kanti's welts but Kanti turned her head away and would not let her.

When Kanti was thirteen, Lalita wanted her to marry a Tandalam cousin. She was desperate for Kanti to escape being a poor relative and wanted her to have a home and status of her own. But even though he was a cross-cousin and not off-limits, Kanti saw him as a brother and refused, for which she was severely beaten by Lalita, beaten until she fainted, but she would not marry him. Luckily, he declared he saw her as a sister and cried off; otherwise it would have been sanctified rape.

Kanti did not like what she saw of her mother's life and that of her eldest aunt, whose Tandalam husband had many liaisons and had sent her away to her father's house to be free of her. This beautiful aunt, whose translucent skin, porcelain features and sweet, soft smile I remember from the 1960s had produced three strapping, handsome and clever sons but even that had not bought her respect and affection in her husband's house for he preferred livelier company. Kanti sensed, too, that many of her aunts, although good and beautiful and doing everything expected of them, were not really happy in their marriages. She decided when she was thirteen that she would never marry.

Kanti loved to draw, paint and embroider but was told by her hostile grandmother that it was a waste of time and money in her case. To feed her eyes, Kanti took to keeping scrapbooks of paintings, poems and pictures of dancers and beautiful people, anything pretty or interesting that caught her eye, cut out from discarded newspapers and magazines. She once tried to embroider a Lakshmi in the style of Raja Ravi Varma's painting at Baroda but something happened to her store of

Two of my favourite magazine clippings from Kanti's scrapbooks—
left: mythological paintings from the 1930s of Shiva Parvati Kalyanam;
right: Jatayu Moksham from the Ramayana.

carefully collected and hoarded embroidery silks and it stayed unfinished. She showed it to me once. I have two of Kanti's crumbling scrapbooks and they are the first things I pack when I move house.

Kanti's hunger for flowers, music, poetry, textiles and art was fed in school. But the foreign nuns in her convent school always spoke ill of Hinduism so she could not trust them with her thoughts and feelings. She shared some of their critical views but did not think it was correct of them, when their own mythology, traditions and history were as questionable, to abuse Hinduism to Hindu schoolgirls who could not answer back. Nor did she find the nuns in sympathy with her strongest feelings, about treating men and women with equal honour and respecting a woman's integrity. She asked Lalita about it and was told that 'God' was probably very different from what those nuns were taught to say and that she should use her own mind.

Kanti also rebelled against having to sing *God Save the King* but the nuns were colonial loyalists and threatened to throw her out of school if she made trouble. In this, too, my father had it easier, for the boys at his school loudly sang '*God shave our gracious King*' with innocent faces and their male teachers looked impassively into the middle distance as though they had not heard.

The freedom movement was gaining ground and Gandhi's views had stirred up the Madras Presidency, the oldest bastion of British rule in India. The uncles were pro-British and disliked political opinions in women so Kanti and Lalita spoke of it softly for Lalita was intensely nationalistic. After being sent back to Sita Sadan, Lalita had set herself to read English, Hindi and Urdu and used part of her scant allowance to buy newspapers in all three languages. She began to keep a secret political diary that Kanti read only after her death. In it, said Kanti, she had poured out all her hopes and apprehensions about the social and political future of the country, its communal rifts and her own absolute abhorrence of caste and gender distinctions. Tripurasundari scoffed at Lalita's reading, especially of English books, but could not really object since Lalita sat down to read only in the afternoon, leaning against a *thoon*, one of the pillars that ran around the inner verandah. She only ever did so after completing any number of household chores. She made good use of Raghavaiyya's library at Sita Sadan and my father and his male cousins would fetch her more books from the Gowri Kumar shelves.

A cousin from Vellore began to visit Sita Sadan in the early 1940s, a well-read and highly intelligent lady who had been married off to a rich but uneducated man. This was surprising in a brahmin but apparently he was not interested in studies. Well-to-do, with acres of paddy, a great many cows, town houses, and gold in vaults, he liked to drink and party with the men of his neighbourhood. His wife, Lalita's cousin, had not been allowed to study and had taught herself to read. She had a keen interest in Marxism and in Lalita she found a kindred spirit. She took to coming over on long visits and she and Lalita would read the Communist Party paper *Janasakti* and secretly procured P. Jeevanandham's Tamil translation of Bhagat Singh's essay *Why I Am An Atheist*, which they had to cover in newspaper to hide from the pro-British uncles. They wanted to visit Mannargudi, near Kumbakonam in the Kaveri Delta, where the first red flag in India was hoisted in 1918 soon after the October Revolution in Russia. But there was no question of the family allowing it.

I thought of Lalita when I went to Mannargudi in 2008 for some pre-Election coverage for *Hindustan Times*, the newspaper I then worked for in Delhi. The Communist Party of India was the oldest political party in Mannargudi and was all-powerful until the 1980s. But though the DMK and AIADMK had taken turns ruling Tamil Nadu since 1967, it was only the late actor-politician M.G. Ramachandran who managed to politically enter this CPI-ruled fortress in 1981 through his personal charisma and free mid-day meal schemes: 'bread and circuses' as the old Roman emperors might have said.

Mannargudi, an old *zamindari* area once known for its rich landlords, was a relaxed and friendly place, 300 km from Madras. It was famous in south India for its medieval Rajagopalaswamy temple to Vishnu and its fine tradition of Carnatic music. But this sleepy temple town, built in a neat grid around a huge, clean open watertank, had contributed fourteen judges to India's highest courts while Needamangalam village next door had contributed a Chief Election Commissioner who had schooled in Mannargudi.

I noticed in my story for the newspaper that

"Though this is a male-dominated traditional society, the mainstream is not a *purdah* culture and the literacy level is 73.5 per cent. Women move about freely with a swing to their hips and a lithe stride. Rural girls cycle to school and back, ribbons fluttering jauntily on their neat, looped plaits. Women go in twos or in girl gangs without a male escort to the cinema for very cheap tickets in the reserved ladies' section—that's another way the actor-politician 'MGR' won over voters. Girls from Mannargudi work in Chennai. For weekends, they take a night bus home in perfect safety. That's the level of security a woman alone enjoys in many parts of south India."

How Lalita and Kanti would have loved that, in place of being immured in the house, I thought. I hoped they were pleased that I, a single, working woman, was skipping about with impunity sixty-plus years later on the edge of rice fields, talking in a friendly, matter-of-fact way to members of the All-India Kisan Sabha or national farmers' union; to the Communist Party of India district secretary who was also the local head of the Panchayat Sabha, representing forty-nine *panchayat* or village administrations; and to a local landowner from an old *zamindari* family. I was spoken to just as cordially and matter-of-factly and invited to tea in their district office and to lunch at their homes.

Though denied travel, Lalita and her cousin spent interesting hours discussing politics at the temple, which was the one place that they could freely visit. It is a piquant thought that these two outwardly meek women sat in a corner of the open courtyard of a temple as the safest place in which to discuss Marxism, atheism and caste. They were joined sometimes by Amiyakka, another brahmin widow, who came to Sita Sadan to help with chores but also managed to teach Kanti and my father a little music through devotional songs set in classical tunes.

Lalita introduced her cousin and Amiyakka to Dr Samuel, the Tamil Christian lady doctor who attended to the women of the family and was locally known as 'Apathikaari Amma', the woman apothecary. I have often wondered if Lalita would have converted to Christianity and gone away from Sita Sadan if she had not had two young children as hostages to fortune. It was Dr Samuel who gave Lalita a picture of Baby Jesus and Mother Mary, which she kept in her *puja* corner. The idea of 'God as Love' must have appealed greatly to Lalita.

Mary was called 'Mariata' in the Tamil lands, which already had an ancient version of the Devi called 'Mariamman' also known as 'Renuka'. Mariamman was a half-dalit, half-brahmin goddess in Tamil Nadu and there was a temple to her in North Arcot where she was worshipped as 'Padai Veedu Amman', the fierce little 'goddess of soldiers'. Dr Ambedkar had even listed an 'impure' caste called 'Renuka' identified with the Mang, Matang or Naam Shudras classified as 'Untouchable' by the British. They were fisherfolk on the coast and were elsewhere considered the first people in India to have harnessed oxen. 'Renuka' was not a name normally given to south Indian brahmin girls but Lalita deliberately chose it for her son's daughter should he have one. There was deep rejection of the cruel old ways in her choice of name for a grand-daughter yet unborn and as I grew older and realised the subversion in Lalita's choice, I felt she was trying to tell me something. I felt close to her, and pleased; pleased with Lalita and pleased with Kausalya, who knew her mythology and Tamil culture backwards and had instantly agreed to name her firstborn that. My father had been a messenger from Lalita to her unknown daughter-in-law who had understood and honoured her intention.

Meanwhile, Kanti had wanted to run away to Gandhi's Wardha Ashram which she then saw as a refuge from the family stranglehold and as a place where she could grow as a person and be part of the nationalist cause. But Lalita had held her back to study and win herself a safe, secure future and Kanti had listened, won over by Lalita's pitiful apology for the beatings. "I was very afraid for you and I'm very sorry I hurt you," Lalita had said and looking at her anxious, sorrowful eyes, Kanti had forgiven her mother.

When my father took Lalita away for good from Sita Sadan to hired lodgings in Madras, Lalita, whose health had begun to fade, took on a dalit couple as part-time help. They ruled the little establishment with a rod of iron for a year until they moved on and were especially tender to Kanti, who said that despite being part of their household, Selvam would only eat food he had cooked himself. I cringed at the thought of the centuries of hurt in that reverse rejection, even of Lalita.

Neither Kanti nor Kausalya kept 'separate' old glasses and plates for their household help and neither did I. They said that it was important to serve them with affection and dignity on proper plates and give them tea in un-chipped cups or glasses; and to refuse beggars nicely with a *namaste* if I had no change to give them. This was not liked by the orthodox families that I had truck with afterwards, but that's how it was. Lalita, Kanti and Kausalya were very much on my mind years later when I invited Bezwada Wilson, founder of the Safai Karmachari Andolan, or movement against manual scavenging, the cleaning of dry toilets by the 'untouchable' caste, to tea at the India International Centre in Delhi. I hoped to persuade him to write for the Religion page in *Hindustan Times,* but he said he was not ready just then.

Like Lalita, Kanti did the unthinkable. After finishing high school with high marks, she wanted to go to college. But the uncles refused to pay for it, insisting that she had to get married and that "anyone would do, even a very poor brahmin." This time Lalita stood by her daughter and turned, not to her brothers, but to her sisters, who had earned their stripes by then in their marriages and were in a position to express an opinion in their homes. One of them slipped Kanti the admission fees. I think it must have been Lalita's elder sister, Manjubhashini, at Gowri Kumar.

But where was the money for tuition and board to come from? Kanti took a cold, clear look at her situation and declared herself a pauper to Madras University; a pauper who had studied hard and had the marks, if not the money, for admission to a BA in Economics in the best colleges. This set off such an uproar that the floors of Sita Sadan must have trembled. An uncle thundered that it was a blot on family honour but Kanti said it was the logical thing to do for a girl who wanted to study and could not pay her fees.

She got her way and went to Queen Mary's College on a government scholarship, staying in the hostel, and went on to do her M.Litt. from co-educational Madras Christian College, which created a bigger uproar. The uncles angrily reproached Lalita for her daughter's rebellion at which Lalita finally protested. What had Kanti actually done, which was so terrible? "She is bound to get entangled with some fellow and there will be a worse scandal," said Lalita's family, which wounded Lalita. Had they no respect for Kanti's integrity? But

Kanti was fighting for her life and nothing would have made her throw it away, certainly not a man.

Kanti had not wanted to go to Presidency College since there were too many male cousins there who would have monitored her and carried tales back. Not that she would have done anything outrageous. She merely wanted to be free to study, to claim the small liberties that any responsible person is entitled to; to come and go from class to library to canteen, walk in the park or on the beach with girls from her class, free of oppressive scrutiny and suspicion. She had a small tin trunk with three plain cotton saris, one to wash, one to wear and one spare; a comb, a bar of soap, a bottle of oil, a toothbrush and a tin of toothpowder, a few notebooks, a pen and a bottle of ink. Her scrapbooks were wrapped up carefully and she had a *paai* or grass mat, a sheet and a small pillow. Her aunts quietly gave her a few *annas* for bus fares.

I don't think Kanti ate well during that time in college but the freedom of those college years put a bloom on her in her twenties. She had not eaten well since childhood, unable to eat properly or with enjoyment in the acrid atmosphere of Tripurasundari's hostility and

Balakrishna Thatha at a concert with Vishali Paati playing the tambura.

had delicate shoulders with the collar bones sticking out, and slender limbs. She put on a little weight and looked relaxed and happy when staying in Gowri Kumar or at Coimbatore with her youngest aunt, Vishali Paati.

Vishali Paati, whom I privately nicknamed 'Despina', the Thorn, for her remarks about my complexion, had a very kind husband, Balakrishna Thatha, a nephew somewhere of the scientist, Sir C.V. Raman, and a wonderful, funny presence in my early childhood. I still remember the children's songs in Tamil that he made up for Kanti and her cousins that I learned in turn from him.

Years after Kanti was dead and gone, Aunt Leela Sekhar found me pictures of her in those years from her own neatly labelled photo albums, capturing the happy times afforded by the Gowri Kumar cousins to the orphans—trips to their fields and coconut groves at Kattamanchi near Chittoor; Kanti in a new sari with her

Kanti at ease on the roof of 'Gowri Kumar'.

aunt Manjubhashini and Uncle Sekhar, all three flanking Leela, the shy new bride of the house; and Uncle Sekhar's British-era holiday cottage, 'Longleat', up in the hills of Coonoor. Kanti was later found to have chronic anaemia whereas my father burst with rude health in comparison. But the luxury of being able to go unfettered to class was beyond anything for Kanti.

The Principal of Madras Christian College was reluctant at first to admit Kanti because the feedback on her was that she had joined the freedom struggle. But her eldest aunt's son, an old student of 'MCC', was in the British Army by then and married to a Syrian Christian lady, which was the first marriage in the clan outside the fold. This big cousin was great-grandfather Raghavaiyya's eldest grandson. It was his mother who had been sent back to Sita Sadan with her three sons by her dissolute Tandalam husband. This cousin was in a good position to vouch for Kanti and she got into MCC. Her tutor, Professor Malcolm Adiseshiah, later recommended her to Oxford for her PhD in agrarian economics at Lady Margaret Hall. K.N. Raj, also a pupil of Professor Adiseshiah, became Kanti's staunch friend and a famous economist in later years.

I remember Kanti's autograph album from the 1940s; it was the western nineteenth century fashion for young ladies at seminaries and colleges to have a little book for mottoes and remembrances from their classmates and famous people. This fashion, which instantly became the rage in British India, carried on right up to my school days. Two Indonesian friends had written '*Merdeka*', 'Freedom', in Kanti's book, which came from the Sanskrit *mahaarthika*, meaning 'rich, prosperous and powerful' in euphemism for 'free'; and there were charming verses in English and Tamil, the Tamil usually a nationalistic verse by Subrahmanya Bharati.

An English friend had written a modified bit of dialogue in Kanti's book from the American Pulitzer winner Louis Bromfield's 1937 novel *The Rains Came* in which colonial and 'new India' tumbled pell-mell together:

"Do you like the French?

"No."

"Do you prefer the English?"

"No,"

"Or perhaps the Russians?"

"No."

"Whom do you like, then?"

"I like my friends."

The inscription was just right for Kanti. Like Lalita, she didn't care about backgrounds, she saw people as individuals, as entities outside the limits of labels.

Kanti enjoyed her three years at Oxford but malnutrition and stress affected her ability to withstand the cold and she fell severely ill with meningitis, during which she grew delirious with high fever and imagined there were huge black spiders coming down the wall to devour her. Nevertheless, she steadied her nerve and submitted her thesis in which she argued that agriculture in India should not be treated merely as a source of raw material for industry but should be developed as an important economic sector itself. This went against the prevailing wisdom of the time that favoured industrial growth above all for India and I believe two 'India experts', Colin Clark and Vera Anstey, rejected her thesis which she had hurried to submit, having lost time because of her illness.

This was a severe blow to Kanti who had no money left and had to go back empty-handed to India to work off her loans. She had joined Miranda House in Delhi

University, having had to refuse an offer from Kinnaird College, Lahore, because of Partition.

Kanti went to London to book her passage home and wandered in the drizzle along the Thames embankment. Lalita was long dead and my parents were busy with their jobs in Calcutta and their first baby, me. Kanti felt that she belonged to nobody and nobody belonged to her. She was back to being poor and alone. Sick with disappointment, exhausted by her long struggle to survive and by her severe illness, she came very close to throwing herself into the cold, grey river. But before that she wanted to do something nice as a salute to life and her Tandalam blood drove her to the theatre. She spent some of her last pounds going to Stratford, to Shakespeare's birthplace, to see Sir John Gielgud in *Othello*.

"It was like ritual enactment," she told me in my teens, "That silly man accepted someone else's word as truth and came to grief. I was damned if I was going to let anyone do that to me. My thesis came to nothing but I had three good years in England because of it, I saw the Lake District and its lovely tarns, I went to Cornwall, to the Yorkshire Dales, saw so many places I liked, I went to

Europe, and I could go home and share my ideas with my students, so all was not lost."

"What happened, then?" I said, giving Kanti a bone-crushing hug for having stayed out of the Thames.

Kanti grinned. "I was fed up with doom and gloom. So I thought I'd treat myself to another show. I saw *Westside Story*," she said.

"That was tragedy, too, it was American *Romeo and Juliet*," I said, taken aback. Kausalya had had a mania for American musicals along with all that Bharata Natyam and I had inherited the dissipation.

"But they sang and danced," said Kanti.

Back in India, Kanti had thrown herself into teaching and after some years, prevailed upon the university to introduce Japanese economic history, which interested her, in the syllabus. She began learning the language at the Japan Cultural Centre. She joined the Delhi Film Society, becoming its Treasurer, and saw a great many classics of world cinema. During the long summer vacations she went with friends from Miranda House to the Himalayan foothills and explored charming British-made hill-resorts like Simla, Naini Tal and Dalhousie. They went up by train and bus and stayed at small, quaint nineteenth-century lodges and guest houses, walked, boated, read, and plotted little excursions to local beauty spots, instinctively avoiding pilgrim traffic.

Kanti sometimes sent me postcards from all kinds of places that she had stockpiled from England and her 'Grand Tour' of Europe. I got Elizabeth the First's Armada portrait from Woburn Abbey once and very fine it looked, stuck on my mirror. I loved lakes, rivers and the sea with a deep, mute love and collected seashells with a yearning I could not explain. Kanti called me her seabird and said she was a hill-mynah herself although she never squawked. Her low-pitched, accent-less voice was very pleasant, turning sometimes to an amused drawl that I can still hear in my head.

Kanti and her friend Uma Chakravarti from the History Department in Miranda House took part in projects of a practical nature over the years, like volunteering to collect funds for pump sets in 1968 as the college contribution to the drought in Bihar.

A glimpse of south India appeared in Delhi occasionally, as in the *Aandal Thiruppavai* ballet by Kalakshetra in the early 1970s, which Kanti took Uma to see. Like Kanti, Uma preferred Indian ballets to

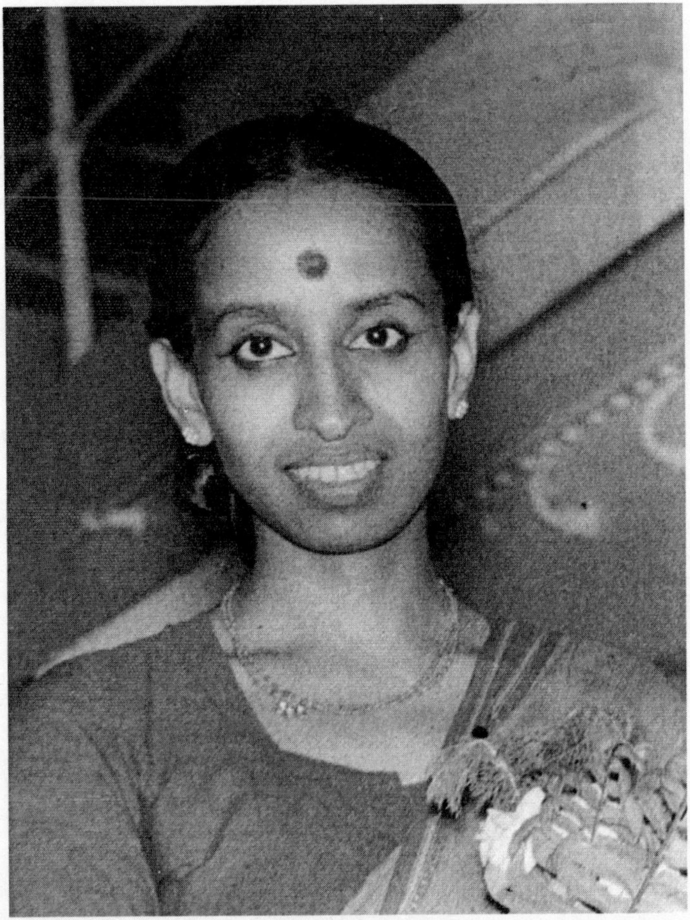

Kanti back in Miranda House from Oxford.

Uma Chakravarti, extreme left, second row, and Miranda House colleagues at a college event in the late 1960s.

solo dances for their theatre. Uma loved her newfound taste for cinema, which she told me was Kanti's doing and Kanti enjoyed visiting Uma, her husband and their young family at their home on campus.

Kanti had joined the Left when she came to Delhi

but had quit in protest in 1956 when the Soviet Union invaded Hungary, although she abided by a number of the better Left principles to the end of her days. Miranda House had a lively tradition of annual class picnics and the girls in the BA Honours courses had a marvelous time of it. They could not go without a teacher and made sure to inveigle their favourites to come along. Kanti noticed that unlike the dashing Honours girls, the low key BA Pass Course girls never went anywhere and nobody took them on picnics. So she offered to go and they had a wonderful day out at Surajkund, at Prithiviraj's old pond, except that Kanti slipped and took a bad fall. It had dire consequences but Kanti was very happy that day to have gone out with the Pass Course students about whom the Honours students were sometimes unkind for being less 'cool', not always understanding how many battles had been fought and won in deeply conservative homes for the girls to get to college at all.

The outwardly fashionable did not entirely own the world as I realised in my time at Miranda House, when I chose Tamil as my Modern Indian Language subsidiary although I had never formally studied it. My reward was the discovery of Ms M. Vasuki, the lone Tamil lecturer in Miranda House. I was in over my head reading the long epic *Pandiyan Parisu* by the modern revolutionary poet Bharatidasan and *Islamiya Bhakti Paadalgal*, Muslim devotional poems in Tamil, but no more than I had been in the last year of school in Delhi, struggling with the Hindi novel *Gaban* by Munshi Premchand.

My father called me a lemming, hurling myself down cliffs to certain doom. But opting for Tamil was my way, I realised, of making my lost mother part of my college life. Kausalya had chosen Tamil over Sanskrit in college, which had so enraged Thatha's orthodox mother that she refused to speak to Kausalya for three days. But Thatha and Ponni had stood by their daughter's choice; on principle and because they loved Tamil themselves, for its hidden harmonies and fluid rhythms in which the first syllables of the lines in a poem rhymed, not the last. Ms Vasuki thus kept a side of me fed and watered that pined deeply for lost Carnatic heritage although I did not fit in with the 'typical' south Indian brahmins I occasionally encountered in Delhi. I was far too westernised to live in their pocket and be subject to their taboos, too fond of things in Delhi, in Bombay, in Baroda, in Calcutta. I wanted Carnatica, I wanted it all, but on easy, pleasant terms, my terms.

Kanti told me that Ms Vasuki was a child widow who had been encouraged to make something of herself by enlightened Mudaliar philanthropists in Madras. She had devoted herself to the study of Tamil literature and had come north for the relative freedom and anonymity of Delhi University. Ms Vasuki was very quiet and unassuming and wholly unfashionable as Honours students understood it but she had treasures to share, and after a while, nice lunches that she cooked herself on a small stove. Her room to the left of the Quad became a haven. I worked harder at Tamil than at any other subject and still got terrible marks but several poems stayed in my head and the love of the language. I was very sorry when Ms Vasuki suddenly died and Kanti said it was worth something to a teacher that "even a feckless dreamer mourned her".

Several years later Kanti was deeply touched when her colleagues unitedly fought and won against a hostile college Principal to get her her entitled year's extension when she turned sixty, arguing that Kanti's physical disability had nothing to do with her sharp mind as a teacher. Kanti had waited patiently in her wheelchair between classes in the corridor in those last few years in Miranda House, unable to climb to the staff room or even walk, because of her hurt leg and the onset of arthritis.

But the corridor was where she made friends with the humbler, shyer girls in college who were not the daughters of India's privilegentsia and lacked their easy social graces, their clipped vowels and advantages of birth and education. Seeing her smile, the girls took to stopping by her side and soon looked for her. They told her about themselves and sometimes asked her to tell them how to persuade a difficult parent or grandparent to let them study further and not force them to marry at seventeen and eighteen.

They brought Kanti tokens of affection; a sprig of jasmine, a long-stemmed rose in cellophane on her birthday, phials of pure rose water from Pushkar in Rajasthan to mix with cold water and cool her face with in summer, flowered cotton hankies, their mother's special *parathas*, a piece of birthday cake. "For you, Ma'am," they said and sometimes, very carefully, they held her frail, twisted hands in their young, strong ones or fought good-naturedly about who would wheel Kanti to her next class, telling Veluswamy in Administration who was very attached to Kanti and knew her timetable to the minute that they would look after Ms Sastri. Veluswamy went along anyway to keep an eye. He had asked Kanti to think of a name for his baby daughter and Kanti had suggested 'Amuda', meaning 'love' in old Tamil. Not only had he and his wife been delighted, the name had won approval for its classical beauty with his elders in Tamil Nadu.

Unlike Kanti whose every step forward had been a struggle and paid for with heavy personal price, my father had sailed with congratulatory words and handshakes and backslapping from the uncles and cousins into Madras Christian College and, needless to say, he was better equipped than Kanti was. The uncles had given him enough, nothing splendid but all very respectable. And what had his college days been like at MCC and Bapatla? "Oh, good fun," said my father. He had found his sister's political views "boring", he told me, and said she was "bitter and angry" which did not sound like the Kanti that I or her friends and students knew. Stung, I asked him how he might have felt in her place and he said, "I don't know why she got so worked up. *I* was a very happy person."

Perhaps he was just being true to the type of Indian man who was conditioned by the centuries to justify his self-centredness by not acknowledging the exploitation of women. This type, to which neither Raghavaiyya nor Thatha had subscribed had acquired prehistoric proportions in my mind as a troglodyte who unaccountably read the classics. How very different it had all been for Kausalya because of her father.

- *Seven* -

Encouraged by Thatha, Kausalya had plunged headlong into the Indian Customs and Central Excise service, the first woman to breach that particular male bastion. One of her reporting officers, a south Indian man, once concluded her annual confidential report with, "She has all the weaknesses of a woman." He had then drawn a thin line through the sentence so that it stayed perfectly legible. His personal assistant who disliked him and respected my mother was shocked by this duplicity and had chosen to break the rules by showing it to her, to warn her of possible career repercussions. She thanked him and went on with her work as though nothing had happened. What could she have done at that point anyway except keep working and hope that it would add up? My father told me about this, years after her death.

My mother had another boss, a no-nonsense, fair-minded Sikh gentleman who had a good opinion of her as an upright, hardworking officer who neither played politics nor crossed the line while not being afraid to take a principled stand. The Sikh boss considered her a good officer, said my father, never mind being a 'woman officer'. Officers of the Government of India have to have their name boards in both Hindi and English on their office door. The Hindi initials of the south Indian who had maligned my mother read '*Chu. Thi. Aa.*' that unfortunately added up to 'idiot' in Hindi in an offensive way. It was certainly not a term for polite company. My mother's Sikh boss took to loudly calling out in the busy office corridor, "Where is Chu. Thi. Aa. ----?". He said it without saying it, the punishment fitting the crime according to his lights. My mother neither laughed nor appeared to notice but carried on serenely, said my father. I thought she must have been glad that some colleagues stood by her.

She generally got on well with her male colleagues who, as any group does with a newcomer, observed her for a while before making up their minds. She was as careful in forming her impressions of them. When she felt she had built up a good track record and a good reputation, it seems she felt comfortable enough to go out with some of her colleagues to lunch. I remember her saying she had gone to a Chinese restaurant called Frederick's in Bombay, so she was probably among the first people in India to eat that signature Indian-Chinese invention at Frederick's, 'Gobi Manchurian'. Her lunch buddies at work were from Calcutta, Shillong and Delhi. My father, for all his westernised ways, preferred traditional south Indian and north Indian food so my mother enjoyed her Chinese lunches with her colleagues. Pretty good for the 1960s and early 1970s, I thought in later years. They had evidently respected my mother's integrity as a woman and did not speak ill of her friendship with her male colleagues. I was told that my mother, in turn, was friendly but not familiar. Her *adakkam* was her armour and a married woman won huge subliminal points in Indian society. A single woman had to be trebly careful.

It seems my mother created a bit of a first in Indian Customs by authorising the search of a diplomat's baggage. He was a senior officer at an important western embassy and very self-assured about his status and his immunity. None of the 'competent authorities' as the term went for officers at the relevant level, liked to deal with him for fear of repercussions from Delhi although they had their reasons for wanting to order his luggage searched. I never learned what those reasons were but I heard from my father years after her death that my mother was told to authorise it and she had, dealing politely but firmly with the offended diplomat. He complained, as expected, and Delhi asked questions of Bombay. My mother's department staunchly backed her for having handled it with relentless politeness. They must have tested her in various ways, I thought, to see if she had what it took to be an officer despite being a woman.

These oral histories were naturally very interesting to me, as was the story that my mother had initially been selected for the Indian Police Service. But it seems C. Rajagopalachari, the first Indian Governor-General of India after the British left, was not in favour of it. My mother knew she had to set a good example as the 'outsider' in a tough world in whichever service she was accepted in and happily joined the Indian Revenue Service. Such stories gave me perspective in later years to keep working steadily through some interesting experiences of my own on a diplomatic assignment, and like Kausalya, I was lucky to find some supportive colleagues.

Ponni told me that my mother had "one last, glorious performance" as a dancer and never looked back although sometimes her eyes would overflow at a dance recital. Indrani Rahman told me, "We never forgave Kausalya for giving up dance." This was in 1975 and Kausalya had been dead two years. Indrani, whom I had seen dancing in Bombay sitting next to my mother, was as kind as she was beautiful. She had come to dance Odissi at Miranda House, enchanting in turquoise silk. After the show, I made my way backstage and thanked her, quavering a little, for her dancing. She spoke gently and affectionately, kindling for that glowing moment the beauty and joy that had meant Kausalya.

Nearly forty years after Kausalya's death I chanced upon the recollections of a former Director-General of the Directorate of Revenue Intelligence, that shadow world depicted in Bollywood as midnight calls from informers, secret files and revenue officers setting out in swift launches after smugglers of guns, drugs and illegal money. He said of India's women revenue officers, "The first name that comes to mind is that of Mrs. Kausalya Narayanan. As she entered the service in the early Fifties, the aspect of integrity need not even be mentioned in

Kausalya in silhouette on the shores of the Arabian Sea at Bombay for a special photo shoot.

her case. She was knowledgeable, a gentlewoman and yet very effective and gave no hint that being a woman had in any way handicapped her even in those days when very few women occupied important positions in services. She was perhaps the first lady to enter Indian Customs and Central Excise Service. If she had not died in that air accident in the early Seventies, in all likelihood she could have gone on to head the service, and the department would not have had to wait for more than two decades for that to happen. She was a worthy predecessor of some able lady officers to follow." It was fascinating to find this recollection about that once-upon-a-time entity in India's vast administrative 'steel frame' who happened to be my mother.

My mother had begun in Madras as a probationer and gone on to serve at Calcutta and Bombay before her first posting as Collector at Cochin. She had stayed for the full two years instead of asking to be transferred within a year as wagered by her colleagues, for the Cochin Collectorate had a very strong trade union profile and nobody there had ever reported to a woman. But she felt comfortable enough with her colleagues to joke at her office farewell that she had "felt quite like Tarzan, with a

Customs House, Cochin, on Willingdon Island.

A Madrasi Memoir
RENUKA NARAYANAN
Chapter 7

lion springing out one moment and a tiger the next," and they had laughed together.

Kausalya was never afraid of falling overboard when she went out on choppy seas on a small Customs launch, to say, the Farewell Buoy, the last buoy out in the Arabian Sea from Cochin harbour, dressed, of course, in a sari as was the rule those days for lady officers. Her many years as a dancer had made her physically confident and given her a good sense of balance on deck. "And if I do fall into the sea," she laughed, "My Toothukodi boys will fish me out," meaning the men from Tuticorin on the Tamil coast, known for its pearl divers, who were posted in Cochin. My mother shared her colleagues' love of the open sea, coming back with thrilling reports of dolphins and big waves and rainclouds massed on the horizon that really looked like the advancing war elephants of classical poetry.

Her next posting as Collector of Customs and Central Excise was to Madras and her city welcomed her back with flowers, parties, invitations to cut ribbons, preside over art events and a lot of attention from the press. It must have all been rather wonderful, a sense of 'something attempted, something done'. Forty-two years after Kausalya's death, when I was invited to speak about 'Reading Religion' in *The Hindu* Literary Festival, I found myself spouting verses by Avvai to the audience. It was utterly epiphanic to be invited to my lost paradise by that historic old newspaper and to speak Avvai's verses aloud in Madras.

The British Consulate in Madras had invited my mother to HM the Queen's birthday reception. I thought of my mother going to that party in Madras and of great-grandfather Raghavaiyya going to the Delhi Durbar

My mother at an office event in Cochin.

reception in Chittoor, when I was invited to the Queen's birthday reception in Delhi years later as an editor—a lawyer in 1911, a bureaucrat in 1973 and a journalist in the twenty-first century. I was deeply rooted in Indian culture and extremely grateful to be a free citizen. But credit where credit was due. It was the English language and the new world it had brought with it that had taken us forward in life and given us a living and an identity since the nineteenth century; and given the Tandalams a living and an identity since the time that Parshuram Sastri had translated the *Dharma Sastras* for the East India Company. I celebrated the Pallavas and Cholas for their ancient works and days but it was the English who had been my particular beneficiaries through their influence on the men of my family. I could not help feeling glad that the *parangi* had come to south India just as fervently as I was glad they were gone.

The British, who had first made a commercial settlement in my ancestral region in 1613 and built Fort St George in 1639, had formed the Madras Presidency in 1654. They had begun to collect 'sea customs' at Madras in 1677. The history of Madras Customs included Elihu Yale, the Marquess of Wellesley and Edward Clive, the somewhat feeble son of Clive of Plassey. The post and its mandate had evolved and the first fully authorised 'Collector of Customs' of Madras had been a Walter Balfour in 1801.

I went to the Madras Customs House in the 1990s to see my mother's portrait in the conference room, paid for after her death with a fund collected by her colleagues. There was a board in the Collector's office with the names of previous Collectors of Customs, Madras. It began with Walter Balfour in 1801 and a long line of male names followed, changing from English to Indian in the late 1940s and suddenly, in 1973, there was a woman's name.

It had suited my mother, I realised, to marry someone like my father whose only close family was Kanti, herself an independent working woman. My father had no money. But he had a steady, respectable job, also in the revenue service, which, with his very westernised outlook had added up to a package that spelt freedom for my mother. She could not have gone back into the box, forced to submit to traditional expectations; for instance, she was always being told by some woman, "I'm sure your children feel neglected," which we did not. We were proud of our dashing mother.

A wedding photo of my parents.

Looking back, I am able to see that Kausalya had gone about it with great thought. She was always afraid that my father might resent it if she got promoted ahead of him, said Rajam in later years, since those days people moved up faster in my mother's department than in my father's. My mother made my father so comfortable that she disarmed him completely. She displayed enough tradition to keep society happy, keeping the thought of the goddess for herself in her daily prayers. And then she had turned right around, with no objections from anybody, and sat late into the night with her colleagues in the weeks preceding the Annual Budget, at Customs House in Apollo Bunder in Bombay and in her other offices, doing her bit to compute India's home earnings since more than eighty per cent of the central government's income came from Central Excise.

My mother, I realised, had been a twentieth century woman with a goal. She was a genuinely warm-hearted and down-to-earth person with no airs. She had a natural refinement, like Kanti, and spoke courteously to everyone. Especially, she never told off subordinates in public but called them to her room to be spoken to. She was also a realist. She played the long game patiently and with great effort and detail, going about it with finesse that betrayed her complete recognition of the world's ways.

I thought that great-grandfather Raghavaiyya, Thatha and Kausalya had a lot in common, packaging themselves right for their times, building buffers that allowed them social and professional freedom, playing along with tradition in some things to pacify the critics and gradually take them along, but never losing focus on their personal goal, which was to get a meaningful life that made them feel part of progress, of moving forward and not stagnating. It was not 'cunning', it was intelligence, driven by the pride and satisfaction of being part of India's effort to stand tall and take her rightful place in the world.

To move from the unorganised world of dance to the world of public administration with its assured benefits and the chance to live in different parts of our vast country must have made absolute sense to a bright young woman. It was Thatha who had held the door open to dance and government service, both unconventional choices then for a woman; Thatha, with his independent views, who had asked his three daughters what they wished to do. My mother had taken the bait and put in the hard work needed for both personas, as a dancer and as a bureaucrat. Ponni had supported Thatha and Kausalya with all her heart. Her father, too, had pushed her to school and into the modern age and she had entered new worlds through reading Hindi and English while also working as a wife and mother and managing her home. They had all committed themselves to change.

What did my mother do for creative satisfaction, though, once she gave up dancing? She wrote. Three published novels in Tamil as 'G. Kausalya'—*Rajayogam,*

The last photograph of my mother as Collector of Customs and Central Excise, Madras.

Griharani and *Dr Akhila,* which was translated into Kannada, about the changing lives of Indian women; a number of short stories for Tamil magazines, articles on dance in English, and when expecting me, she published an illustrated series on Bharata Natyam in a Tamil magazine, called *Natya Anubhavangal*, 'Dance Experiences', posing for the pictures herself before it was too late. She wrote sometimes for *The Illustrated Weekly of India* in the 1960s, said my father, unable to remember the dates. I remembered the small white van of *The Times of India* though. If I saw it while playing downstairs, turning in from Pedder Road into the 'Dharbanga Mansions' lane where we lived, I was almost always sure that it was headed to our building to collect an article written by my mother.

The dance world had not let go of Kausalya. I remembered a Saturday morning at Darbhanga

Mansions. I was outside playing hopscotch when a slim young man and a glowing young goddess accosted me. "Can you tell us where Srimati Kausalya Narayanan lives?" the man asked. It was the young dance journalist Sunil Kothari and the goddess was Sonal Pakvasa, later Sonal Mansingh, the renowned Odissi dancer, who had come by to chat about the dance with my mother.

A lively, pretty girl called Rasika Khanna had come by one day to my mother's house on Willingdon Island, Cochin, when on a visit to her friend down the lane, the daughter of Admiral Menon. Rasika was a Bharata Natyam student at Kalakshetra in Madras and the daughter of the Delhi-based painter Krishen Khanna.

Her mother, also a Renuka, told me years later in Delhi that on their first visit to Madras in the late 1940s, their friend, the aesthete and arts administrator Dr Narayana Menon, had promised that he would introduce them to Bharata Natyam. He had taken them to see my mother dance at the Museum Theatre. "It was our first glimpse of the dance," said Renuka Khanna. "I can still see what Kausalya wore; I can see her movements in my mind's eye."

The cover of one of my mother's Tamil novels, "Dr Akhila."

As kind as Indrani, I thought, soft-hearted women giving something back of a dead mother to her daughter. Dr Kapila Vatsyayan, the famous arts scholar, told me when I was Arts Editor, *The Indian Express* that she had actually photographed my mother in dance class with Pandanallur Chokkalingam Pillai in the 1940s but could not remember where the photographs were. "I know I'll suddenly find them one day and I'll give them to you then," she said.

I was overcome when the great mridangam maestro, Dr Umayalapuram Sivaraman, told me one year that he remembered my mother very well, that "Kausalya had that perfection, she was a very fine dancer." A story told by Ponni came to mind after that, about the legendary Carnatic flute maestro, 'Maali' or T.R. Mahalingam. It seemed he reserved or bought several seats in the front row for my mother's performances and would mark the *taalam* or beats when she danced *jatis*, the complicated rhythmic passages of the dance. "But she was totally absorbed in her dancing and the only person who existed for her was her guru, Pandanallur Chokkalingam Pillai, she was his pupil for twelve years," Ponni had said.

Kausalya in her 'cover girl' days in Madras in the 1940s.

I knew that my mother had called him 'Vadyar', Tamil for 'Teacher' and sometimes he had called her 'drumstick'. She had taken me to meet him at a felicitation ceremony in Bombay in July 1965. The souvenir had wonderful bits of history in it. Messages, from the great dance activist E. Krishna Iyer, from Rukmini Devi of Kalakshetra, from the beautiful dancer-actress Vyjayanthimala, from the eminent musicologist Dr V. Raghavan, then the Honorary Secretary of the Music Academy, Madras, from a famous art critic of those years, Charles Fabri, who had once told Kanti in Delhi that she had "Vaigai eyes", Vaigai being the river in the ancient Tamil city of Madurai; and photographs of the Pandanallur pupils of that time, Mrinalini Sarabhai, Indrani Rehman, Kausalya and Ritha Devi of the Tagore family. Exquisite Alarmel Valli was to be his last great pupil.

My mother had written a tribute to her guru in that souvenir praising his detachment, his "indifference to fame and fortune", that there was "no playing to the gallery" and about the joy of learning, the joy of dancing. Especially, she said, "I have never heard Vadyar make an unkind remark about any other teacher of the art," and that "his sincerity and infinite patience touched us like a

'Vadyar' (white-haired, fourth from left) conducting a dance performance by my mother in Madras.

magic wand, brushing away the agony and frustration of long hours of relentless practice, making us as eager for the next lesson as for the first." She made me do a proper dancer's salute to him, which I executed as gracefully as could be expected from a girl who preferred reading to running. Her guru blessed me with a noticeable twinkle in his eye and told my mother in Tamil, "She's becoming a little potato. Tie up that chubby waist, make her exercise more." It was so kindly said that I grinned, "Quite shamelessly," said my mother to my father on the way home.

Kausalya's home had been very simple and more 'south Indian' than Kanti's with a couple of embellished Ravi Varma prints in dark wooden frames, a couple of Tanjore paintings, a few fine grass mats, little Chola-style bronzes, brass vases, a planter's chair, and a few painted wooden boxes and toys from Kondapalli in our room. I was very attached to a stylised *paachi*, a typical wooden doll from Tamil Nadu, and liked to dress it in strips of cloth left over from the skirts and frocks made for me by a tailor who would install himself every now and then on the balcony in Bombay or at the back of the house in Cochin with my mother's sewing machine.

My mother did not like clutter. Her homes had many bookshelves though and solid elephant book-ends in teak. She had frosted jugs and glasses from the 1950s with plain powder blue plates for company and stainless steel for everyday. Shc chose a dinner service with a geometric, not floral, design from the Alwaye Potteries in Kerala. We could not touch her writing corner but the flats we lived in, and later, her bungalow as Collector of Customs, Cochin, gave three active children as much space as possible.

Fresh coffee beans were roasted and ground in our house every month, *rasam* and *sambar* spices fried, big pots of yoghurt set every day, and my mother tried out new recipes on weekends, which my father dreaded and we loved. The kitchen would smell of vanilla pound cake baking or vegetable pie or vegetable *kormas* and *koftas*. The pickle bottles and *vadaams* and *appalams* never seemed to finish. We had balloons, cakes and streamers for our birthdays, my dolls and books had their own shelves and our games and toys lived in another cupboard.

A visit to the cinema with all three of us meant a big cane basket crammed with cheese and chutney sandwiches, chocolate biscuits and a big flask of orange squash to sustain us through the screening. My father drove us all sometimes in Bombay to the Hanging Gardens, to the Aarey Milk Colony gardens or to Powai Lake and my mother would produce a similar picnic from a woven basket that held everything, even the *jamakalam* or thin, striped cotton *dhurry* typical of Tamil Nadu.

My mother took me to see Tamil films at the Aurora cinema hall in Bombay, hits of the day and splendid mythologicals like *Adi Parasakti* and *Thiruvilayadal,* and I developed a lifelong addiction to Tamil film songs. She spoke to me in code about going to the cinema since she did not want my little brother and sister to set up a howl about being left behind. I feel sorry that my mother missed the new wave of arthouse cinema in the mid-1970s. She would have liked Shyam Benegal's films and Kannada movies like *Chomana Dudi*.

I had my own oval English biscuit tin with a Romney painting on its lid, in which I kept the dainty Jaipuri enamel ear-rings and pendants that Kanti gave me and my *paasi malai*, the colourful bead necklaces sold in Madras by the Lambadi *korava* and *korathi.* These gipsy men and women, originally from Rajasthan, had wandered freely over India until the British declared them a 'Criminal Tribe' in 1871 and curbed their nomadic lifestyle. They were restored to society only in 1952 when the ruling was abolished by independent India and my mother said it was a shame that they had been persecuted in the first place. She liked it that I liked their bead and glass jewellery better than silver or gold and always bought me a necklace or two, a practice I resumed as an adult whenever I visited Madras, just as I made sure to buy white lawn handkerchiefs edged with convent-made lace from the Victoria Technical Institute on Mount Road, for my mother always had one of those in her handbag.

Ponni taught me to say a piece, an imaginary singsong dialogue in Tamil between a *korava* and a *korathi* and it was one of my performance pieces if asked to sing, which sometimes startled south Indian brahmin ladies who expected a devotional song in a classical raga.

I did not dare tell my mother about the rude 'servant song' with sarcastic tonal inflexions that I had learned from our elderly *samayalkara mami* or lady cook, which went: "*O sonny boy, kathrikkai, kaanj pona velrikkai; Velekaari vandiley, roja-poo kondeiley, maatu-paiyyan pakkathley; Dey, ottra vandi, Coachman!"* It was a salty, satirical old verse by Tamils mocking 'brown sahibs'—like us, for instance—as emasculated servants who aped their English masters. Roughly translated, it meant, "O sonny boy, eggplant, dried-up cucumber; the maid sits in the carriage with a rose in her hair, the cowherd by her side, saying 'Hey, drive on, Coachman!'" I now think my mother would have laughed had I told her.

She had taken me to see the Ravi Varma paintings in Trivandrum and before I could turn broody over *Judith* and ask questions, she had dragged me off for another look at *Damayanti and the Swan*. We had fought because I had resisted and said Damayanti looked "smug" and my father said, "He posed her like Romney but the other way," and my mother said I only did it to annoy and that my father and I were both *otta kappal dorai*, 'leaky-ship lords', a rude old Tamil term for Indians who were very anglicised without their ship ever having left the harbour.

Our garden in Cochin reflected her own east-westism, though. My mother had grown several kinds of jasmine and hibiscus, being wholly addicted to both. She had brought back a "green rose" plant from Munnar and planted a *nagalinga* tree on our side lawn and had huge pots of hydrangea in the 'main porch' and spider lilies lining the drive. When we opened our front door, the first thing we saw was masses of flowers.

It was a proper home with everything in it and my mother tried to give us the best of both worlds. Especially, she had accustomed me since my earliest childhood in Calcutta to the luxury of an old-fashioned south Indian oil bath every Sunday morning. In every town we lived in, an old lady would come by to massage me with warm oil, scrub me with powders of green gram and chickpea mixed in milk and wash my hair with *shikakai* herbal paste. She would finally scent my hair with the healing smoke of a sweet-smelling resin called *sambrani* burnt on live coals in a terracotta bowl under a smooth cane hood. I was dressed in soft, fresh cotton clothes before being summoned to a big Sunday lunch that sometimes featured *kandathippili rasam*, a tonic.

The bath, *sambrani* smoke and lunch made me very sleepy as they were meant to and I was despatched for an afternoon nap to a cool, dark room. This restorative routine was meant to refresh me for the next week of school.

My brother and sister on the big balcony of our home on Willingdon Island, Cochin, with Bolghatty Island visible across the water.

They woke me at four in the afternoon with milk, fruit and biscuits and sent me out to play. I had to be home before it began to get dark and my mother had trained me to wash my feet, hands and face as soon as I entered, dry off neatly and go straight to the *puja* room where the brass *Kamakshi-deepam* oil lamp was lit. I had to bow to the gods and recite the *Yakundendu,* a small Sanskrit prayer to Sarasvati and finish any remaining homework at once.

It was dinner time then and on some Sunday evenings, my mother would make all three of us sit in a row on a silky *paai* and feed us from one big plate while she told us a story. I learned to spot the moral and my mother told me to wait for my brother and sister to work it out and not give it away, "to develop their own understanding," she said.

"Never walk the path of darkness yourself but be aware that bad things exist," my mother said on our last Dipavali together in Cochin, in November 1972. My brother and sister were not allowed near fire and we had gone out by ourselves to light the oil lamps edging the drive and on the gateposts and garden wall.

"I don't like the word 'innocence'. It means," my mother said, tapping my head with her knuckles, "In, no sense."

- *Eight* -

It's curious how my mother elaborately observed the Varalakshmi Vratam for my father. I strongly suspect that Thatha did not approve and must have asked my mother why she took on such rituals. Perhaps she said that since my father had been deprived of growing up in his father's home and had only ever seen his beautiful mother in plain, colourless clothes, never celebrating anything in her own right, she was trying to make up a little for it and give him a sense of fullness and festivity in his own home.

My mother had a personal equation with 'God' and was not a ritualist by temperament. So I am convinced that it was to make my orphaned father feel special that she formally observed the Savitri Vratam in March, called Karadayan Nombu in Tamil, and the Varalakshmi Vratam in August, which are ancient rites that married Hindu women observe for the longevity and well-being of their husbands.

My mother called these ritual events her 'slog overs' but since it was an entirely voluntary commitment, she did everything required and more with elan. She could easily have avoided the fuss and bother. There was no older woman at home to compel her to observe the smallest ritual, my father did not really expect it from his modern, working wife and Kanti was outside the pale of organised religion.

Typically, I remember Savitri Vratam or Karadayan Nombu through the *adai* with white butter, simple steamed patties with a hole in the middle, eaten as ritual food in the evening after my mother's day-long fast. They were made of rice flour and roasted, soaked *karamani* or black-eyed peas and had a white salted avatar and a brown one made sweet with jaggery. Both rejoiced in bits of fresh coconut. My mother tied a *manja sharadu* on my wrist, a cotton thread stained lucky yellow with turmeric, to bring me luck as well.

Savitri was the ancient princess who had brought her husband Satyavan back from the dead, subverting the natural laws by tricking the Lord of Death when he came for Satyavan's soul. The story was greatly revered by Hindus. However, the way my mother told me the story with a straight face but with a faint glint in her eye, made me suspicious. Something was not quite right about this story. I thought it over and found that I did not like Savitri at all for her trickery and I found Satyavan uninteresting. Had he been worth the bother? My mother's lips twitched when I asked her but all she said was "Want another *adai*, Solomon?" Kanti was amused when she heard and drawled, "My, my, a mind of her own. And where did you get it, my dear?"

Varalakshmi Vratam, always on a Friday in the month of Shravan in the *shukla paksh* or moon's bright fortnight, was beautiful in our house. This was for the goddess to whom my mother addressed her prayers. She said two Sanskrit prayers to her every evening that I almost knew myself, the *Mahalakshmi Ashtakam* and the *Mahishasura Mardini Stotram*. They were both power prayers and I can hear my mother's sweet, steady voice reciting them.

My mother had a silver mask of Lakshmi, the goddess of fortune, a little bigger than the size of her palm. She tied this to a coconut and placed it face-front in a narrow-necked brass pot about a foot high. She tied

Indicative photo of Varalakshmi Vratam sourced from kind friends in Madras since I have no visual record of it from Kausalya's day.

a little silk apron over the pot, so that the installation looked like a doll in a skirt.

She fixed a long plait of flowers to the doll's back and hung a canopy over it, a fine Benarasi silk stole in iridescent *mayil-kazhutthu* or 'peacock-neck blue'. It looked lovely in our living room and the ritual prayers were done early in the morning to formally install the 'goddess' in our home. We had to hold a little brass plate with lucky red lime water in it and wave it clockwise thrice at our front door, singing "*Raave ma intiki*," 'Come to my house', in Telugu, to the goddess of fortune. This was the North Arcot custom.

My mother had little cards printed in her name and that of her daughters, inviting ladies of her acquaintance to *manjal-kumkumam*, to come and accept lucky turmeric-and-vermilion at our house. The ladies would arrive in the evening, kowtow to the goddess of fortune in our house and sit around on carpets and grass mats on the emptied floor of our living room. Like the other women, my mother wore a silk sari and diamond ear-rings, "the uniform", she chuckled. My little sister and I wore ours, the silk skirt and blouse called *pavadai-chokka*.

Drilled rigorously to neither trip nor drop things,

I had four duties every year at Varalakshmi Vratam between the ages of eight and thirteen. First, to carry around a silver salver with three silver bowls on it, of turmeric paste, vermilion paste and sandalwood paste. I had to bend my knees and extend both arms with the salver at the right height, held steady and straight, to each lady seated on the floor. When every single one had anointed herself, I had to bring the salver back carefully to its designated place and put it down neatly and quietly. My mother made me rehearse this many times until her critical eye was satisfied. I was put on my honour to not disgrace her and myself by being clumsy or careless. I dare say I had my share of mishaps but I don't remember any, just the smooth, cool feel of the salver and how pretty everything looked.

My second duty was to go around with the silver flower-basket. It was filled with strings of jasmine and red roses for each lady to tuck into her hair. The basket was special. It was an engraved token from the Madras Music Academy to my mother for dancing in its annual Season in December 1946.

My third duty was to make several rounds with the tray of *shundal*. These were tiny, brown chickpeas, boiled and spiced with curry leaf and coconut. This was the *prasadam* or blessed food for the event. My mother led this round, carrying the bigger tray with little leaf cups of *shundal* while I followed with a small tray. Collecting empty cups was my follow-up duty. My sister was too little for these tasks and never got to do them at all, for my mother died when she was six years old.

The ladies chatted away and took turns to sing Carnatic songs to the goddess. They looked like goddesses themselves in their soft silk saris, their foreheads bright with lucky marks, diamonds at their ears and throats and pretty bangles on their wrists. The room smelt very pleasantly of flowers and mild sandalwood incense and the redolence of the morning's *puja* ingredients.

I had to look alert and spring to my fourth duty when the ladies began to leave. There was a large inlaid wooden tray placed on a table by the door, neatly piled with little cloth pouches, one for each lady and a few extra. My mother made these up with great care, making sure to buy only those things that were nicely made and attractively packaged. Each pouch held a comb, a tiny mirror or compact-with-mirror, a little round box of *kumkumam*, a piece of dried turmeric root, a few fresh betel leaves with areca nuts and a pure cotton blouse-piece for a sari, in lucky crimson or ochre. My task was to keep handing my mother a pouch for each parting guest. There could be conversational intervals between one pouch and the next as they took leave one by one. I had to make sure I always had a pouch ready for when my mother held out her hand.

My mother was strict about economy of movement. She did not like 'galumphing gals', she said, and her own movements were neat and graceful without being artificial while her step was light and noiseless to the end, even though she had put on weight as the years went by. 'Deportment' was serious business in her book and I was always being told off about bad posture. My father tried once to tell her to "take it easy" but my mother told him politely that she supposed she could bring up her daughter as she wished. My father said I was being trained like a performing monkey and I waited for the sky to fall, "*vaan idunju vizhundhu ponaal bhumilum,*" 'if the sky should split and fall to the ground' as my mother's beloved poet Bharati said. But my mother suddenly looked woebegone. "She *is* a performing monkey, she's a girl," she said in a small voice. I tried asking her about it but was told to get on with Hindi spelling.

I was made to walk in a straight line with two heavy books on my head, *The Concise Oxford Dictionary* and *The Wonder that was India* by A.L. Basham. If the COD was missing in action, my mother pulled out *The Complete Works of Jane Austen*.

We had a black Fiat, a Premier Padmini, and one day I tumbled into the back seat unheeding of my arms and legs. "Out," said my mother conversationally.

I gaped at her.

"Get into the car properly," she said, "Slide in first without a fuss and smoothly pull your legs in, knees together, feet together, at a neat angle, not high, not low. In one smooth movement. Now."

I had to repeat the manoeuver a few times before she said, "That'll do for now," and we could leave.

My aunt Rajam said that I reminded her of a wild animal straining at the leash. My mother laughed. "*Adhu padu sadhu*, it's a very meek child. But a free spirit inside, so she has to learn to be careful. Don't worry, I'll win. I have many more years to work on her," she said.

Where she did not win was in Bharata Natyam class. I learned the dance from my mother and from

Guru Kalyanasundaram Pillai in Bombay and after her death, from Guru Pandanallur Swaminathan Pillai, and Guru Nana Kasar of Triveni Kala Sangam in Delhi. But I was too shy to even think of dancing in public and was content to learn and watch.

My mother was devastated when I proved to be myopic at nine and needed glasses. "What's the use of learning dance," she said, producing a funny face, "You'll go *tai-dhi-ti-tai* in the *tirmanam* and fall off the stage into the chief guest's lap." This was before contact lenses had caught on and I felt wretched to have disappointed her. She cheered up a little when Dr Kapoor, my kind eye doctor at Bombay Hospital, said he had never heard a little girl read so well. That earned me a *kulfi* at the Parsi Dairy Farm on Princess Street.

It was very interesting growing up around my mother. She regularly quoted poetry, sang, danced, told funny stories and took me out a lot. She was very fond of the second century Tamil Sangam poet's maxim, "*yaathum oorey, yaavarum keḷir*", 'All towns are our towns, all people are our people,' that she taught me, not only to help me adjust to our moving from Calcutta to Bombay to Cochin but as a worldview and a life code.

We went to many dance performances, concerts, plays and films in Bombay. I watched Sitara Devi dancing, a wild, exciting sight; and beautiful Indrani Rehman, my mother's *guru-behen* or sister-in-dance as fellow-pupil of Chokkalingam Pillai; Yamini Krishnamurti, Vyjayantimala, the Travancore sisters, Kanak Rele, whose depiction of Putana the Child-killer was so convincing that it kept me awake that night, the dainty Jhaveri sisters; every one of the great dancers of the 1960s, divinities all.

While I could be shielded to some extent from tragic epic figures like Sita and Draupadi, there was not the smallest use trying to keep anybody ignorant of Krishna or Ganesha who were everywhere in the air. My mother seemed happily attached to both. A month before Ganesh Chaturthi I was told to save and smooth out toffee wrappers in jewel colours. We had to go choose a small terracotta idol for the day Ganesha 'came to live' in our house for ten days and it was my duty to fashion his *kodai,* his royal umbrella. A perfect circle had to be cut from the cover of an old notebook, a long, thin piece of wood was pierced and glued through its middle for the stem, the whole had to be covered with crepe paper and

Ganesha in the south Indian style.

toffee wrappers and a nice, neat fringe had to be added. I did my best but was aware early in life that I lacked the artistic touch. Nevertheless, my crooked *kodai* was ceremonially presented to Ganesha and mountains of salt and sweet *modak*, called *kozhakattai* in Tamil, were made at home. These delicious steamed dumplings had two versions like the Karadayan Nombu *adai;* a salted lentil filling and a sweet filling of coconut and jaggery. Strangely, someone always fed me *modak* every year after my mother's death, they arrived just like that out of the blue and I even grew to expect it just like a bit of rain was always expected on Janmashtami.

Krishna's birthday, Janmashtami, was my mother's favourite festival. I never got around to asking her why but the happiness around it was like sweet liquor in my veins. Years later, my first sip of Tokay, the sweet dessert wine of Hungary, made me blink in surprise. There was a delicacy and a freshness, yet fullness, to the taste of Tokay that seemed exactly like the spirit of Janmashtami in childhood, before I was old enough to read the epics critically. Janmashtami began in our house with the churning of fresh white butter. My mother mixed a great ball of white butter with sugar and put it on a plain, round silver plate. She took this to our *puja* room to the Navaneeta Krishna, a tiny bronze idol of Krishna the Butter-thief crawling as a baby on hands and knees. She lit an oil lamp, offered flowers and put the butter plate gently near the idol.

I had to sing and dance for the Holy Child with my mother keeping time. We had two songs in Tamil first, '*Teerada vilayattu pillai*,' and '*Mangaiyargal*' about Krishna's pranks as a child. This was followed by a song of praise in Sanskrit, '*Gokula nilaya kripalaya palaya, Goverdhana Giridhari Muralidhara*' with my mother prompting. This song was special; it had my sister's name in it in the next line, '*Neeraja nayana neeradhi sayana*,' 'Lotus-eyed one, at rest on the ocean'. After I begged a little, my mother would sing and even dance. I can see her hand forming the *suchi mudra*, the *pathaka* and the lotus *mudra*.

Before the singing and dancing, my mother mixed white rice-flour with water to make a thin batter and we took it to our front door. She drew a fine *kolam* first in welcome outside the door. I was taught to quickly dip three finger tips and the tip of my thumb in the batter and make stylised prints of 'baby toes' one after the other

This is the photo I keep framed of Kausalya for the glimpse of her hand.

on the freshly cleaned and dried floor, cleaned with a fresh, new cloth. The 'footprints' led from our front door to the living room, through the corridors and into the *puja* room, to the butter plate amidst the flowers. This was to welcome Baby Krishna into our house, whenever the Blue God chose to drop by, and his favourite food, fresh, white butter, was waiting for him when he did.

"Will he really come to eat it?" I had asked excitedly when I was six.

"It's a lovely thought," my mother had said. "Just suppose it were all true?"

"Won't he come to our house?" I persisted.

"We don't know God's ways," said my mother, "but at least we'll know we said 'Thank you for everything.' Think of these things as greeting-cards to God, small, pretty ways of saying thanks."

I often thought of that after my mother's death when a disconnect developed between my father and my aunts. When my mother was due to be transferred to Madras from Cochin, she wanted me to finish Class Ten, my last year of school at St. Theresa's, as a boarder before I came to live with her in Madras for my 'pre-University' year and college education. She put my brother and sister into boarding schools in the Shevaroy Hills in Tamil Nadu; my brother at Montfort Boys' High School and my sister at the Sacred Heart Convent for Girls. We had been boarders for nearly three months and quite liked it. My mother sent me news of my brother and sister and wrote me cheerful, funny letters, and the teachers and girls were very nice to me. I missed my mother but knew it was only for a year and looked forward to Madras. I got very good grades in school and my mother was very pleased.

I was sent to Bangalore for the Easter holidays, where my mother came to see me one weekend from Madras. She took me shopping to Brigade Road for jeans and tops and also bought a lurid blue daisy-printed skirt that I wanted the moment I saw it. She went back to Madras full of lovely plans for our life there, leaving me to go back to Cochin. My last sight of her was at Bangalore railway station on her way back to Madras. She had wanted me to try out a 'half-sari' or *davani* before we left "just for fun," she said casually and I had made dreadful faces and said, "Never! In jeans I live and in jeans I die. You won't make me wear it, I know you won't." "Just to disguise yourself a bit at first, Madras won't be like Bombay; it's 'square'," said my mother at her winsome best, all apologetic charm, but with an underlying resolution that promised a few battles. I went back to Cochin and St Theresa's, grinning at the prospect, thinking of how I would argue my case and make her laugh and say, "I give up, Father William." One morning, a few days later, some of her Cochin colleagues came to school and one of them said, "There was a bad air crash in Delhi last night. I'm sorry to have to tell you that Madam was on that flight and did not survive." They had tears in their eyes. The nuns took me back to my dormitory to pack.

Mr Samuel Hallegua and his wife came to see me off at Cochin airport. They were Cochini Jews and friends of my mother's. Mr Hallegua was from Presidency College, Madras, like my mother, and between them they had rounded up others in Cochin; Jews, Christians, Muslims and Hindus, and set up a social group called POSH for 'Presidency Old Students Hodge-Podge'. They had dinners at each other's house with their wives and husbands, and exchanged stories, played word games and had very pleasant times together.

My mother also had great regard for Mr and Mrs K.M. Mathew of the *Malayala Manorama* newspaper group and Mrs Annamma Mathew, who was a terrific cook and had published many cookbooks, had given my mother some. My mother enjoyed trying out her recipes for vegetables, rice and puddings and cakes and also had a few Moplah recipes written down. Our housekeeper in Cochin, an elderly brahmin widow from Madurai, refused to stay if we cooked meat at home and my mother who was vegetarian herself but let us eat everything, had charmed the old lady into making us *parathas* and egg curry, Moplah-style, from these recipes. I could hear my mother laughing at us as we ate everything on our plates. The old lady beamed when my mother asked her to see for herself what a wonderful cook she was.

I could hear my mother's office driver Parameshwaran Nair sternly telling me not to sit next to the Malabar Hotel's cabaret dancer on the waterbus from Willingdon Island where we lived to the mainland part of Cochin, Ernakulam, where my school was. I had made a beeline for her the previous day because she seemed like a nice girl and looked so interesting and different from the other ladies on the boat. Word had got back at once that the Collector's daughter was getting very friendly with the cabaret dancer; so Parameshwaran Nair was taking steps of his own to save our collective honour.

I saw Mani, our own driver, a kind, protective young man who got us bags of greens for our rabbits, Samson and Delilah, in their big hutch in our back garden. My mother grumbled at having to clean their hutch because I often forgot, with my nose in a book, although the deal was that I had to look after pets myself and not leave the messy jobs for others.

I saw Rukmini, our maid, running frantically after me to the jetty to stop me from getting into the fish-seller's boat for a ride to Bolghatty Island across the harbour channel. The island, with its fine Dutch palace, belonged to the Navy and Rear-Admiral Kamat played golf there. He had invited my parents to lunch and I was so upset at not being invited too that I had asked to be taken across on my own, "not for lunch, just to go on the boat," I swore in tears when hauled back.

I saw myself on the scaly branch of the guava tree in our big back garden, munching an apple and reading *The Famous Five*. I saw my mother in an old sari, grubbing in the vegetable patch with the gardener, making plans for tomato chutney and pickled brinjal, and all of them shouting at me to stay out of the way when coconuts were being knocked down from the six bountiful trees in the back garden.

Saying good-bye to Mr and Mrs Hallegua that rainy morning, it was difficult to properly understand that I was leaving south India, home no longer, my mother and our life with her gone forever. I'd worn my new clothes from Bangalore, my mother's last present, to leave Cochin in. I was going back to Bangalore, to Uncle Sekhar's house.

My uncle had driven to Yercaud to fetch my brother and sister to Bangalore. He flew with us to Delhi and took us to Kanti's flat in the Miranda House staff quarters at Delhi University. My mother's body, like that of others, was charred beyond recognition so there was a mass funeral at the Lodi Road crematorium that only my father went to after a frantic round of the hospital wards trying to identify her. He went back to Madras after that with my aunt Rajam, gave away most of my mother's things and took a transfer to Delhi to come and live with us in Kanti's flat. The airline collected the debris from the ground and the families were asked to identify the objects. My father came home with my mother's charred *taali*, her golden wedding chain. The goddess medallion on it was charred, too. If we fell sick and she took our temperature, my mother had pressed that medallion on our foreheads before looking at the thermometer reading. My father locked it away. I saw him reading *Eugene Onegin* and suddenly closing the book and going out for a walk.

A few weeks after we came to live with Kanti, my father startled us all by suddenly ordering me to wash and dress my brother and sister every day for school, oil and comb their hair, babysit them when they came back from school and do their homework with them. "I can do some of it but not everything," I protested. "Who'll do my homework then? I've joined school here in the middle of the year and the syllabus is completely different in Delhi. I'll need a tutor for Hindi; it's too advanced for me. And when will I get free time to read?"

"That's too much responsibility for a schoolgirl in her position," protested Kanti, "you'll need to do some of it yourself." My father ignored her. "You are a very selfish girl and I'm disappointed in you," he said coldly and our paths diverged from that point.

It took me some time to realise that my father had gone back in his head to the Sita Sadan of the 1930s and what his mother and sister had done—doing all the chores while he had been left completely free to play or read, coming home only to eat and sleep like his father had before him. It was the life he had led with my mother, too. But while the grannies were married at thirteen and Kanti had never married at all, my mother married at twenty-seven and had had me only a fortnight before she turned thirty.

Kausalya had employed a cook-housekeeper and two babysitters in Bombay, one for my brother and one for my sister. She usually called just as I walked in from school and I would race straight from the door to the phone, dropping my satchel as I ran, to tell her about my day. Every year when my prep leave began for the annual exams, she asked her boss if she could bring me to the office to study.

Her room in Customs House had a screened-off portion with a table, a chair and a lamp. I sat very quietly there to revise, happy to be near my mother all day. She had lunch with me, made me walk around the room to stretch my legs and sent me back in to study. I had biscuits and lemon barley water to hand and could take a short nap when tired. I never made a sound and if she went away for meetings, I stayed peacefully in *purdah*, studying. Her colleagues called me 'Casabianca' after the boy who "stood on the burning deck when all but he had fled". Sometimes, they sent over a little Cadbury bar "to help me study," smiled the peon who delivered it to 'Baby'. Sometimes, when my father picked us up in the evening, she would take me to Satkar's Restaurant at Churchgate for a snack or to Akbarally's shop for my favourite mutton-and-egg rolls that I ate in the car on the way home.

My grannies had worn saris and had a wedding chain around their necks at thirteen. I wore *pavadai-chokka* only for ritual events. Otherwise I only ever wore jeans or short cotton skirts and frocks, and pointed white zip-up boots to school in the monsoon. When I was transferred from Hill Grange High School in Bombay, to St Theresa's in Cochin, the nuns had asked my mother to make my skirts and frocks much longer, to well below the knee. But I had continued to jump in and out of puddles, hang my turquoise duckback raincoat on its appointed hook and let our housekeeper dry the tartan-printed insides of my rainboots with my mother's Braun hair-dryer.

Kausalya had hired Mani in Cochin to take us to school in our own car on rainy days and maintained another set of minders to be with my brother and sister. She got me my first and only puppy, a black Labrador that I named Inky and it was my job to look after him before and after school and gently clean the corners of his eyes with cotton wool dipped in mild potassium permanganate solution when they got oozy. But when her transfer order to Madras arrived, Inky, still a puppy, went back to the people he came from for my mother had decided to send us all to boarding school. The Collector's Bungalow in Madras was being renovated and she planned to stay in the guest house on the top floor of Madras Customs House until it was ready. She had bought a plot of land on Beach Road near Kalakshetra, paying off the mortgage on a bank loan. Nudged by her, her sister Rajam and her friend Prema Raghavan had bought the plots on either side of ours and my mother had looked forward to making a home for us in Madras.

My mother promised me a nice room and bathroom of my own, lots of bookshelves and a balcony overlooking the garden. We had walked on the quiet waterfront at sunset outside our home on Willingdon Island in Cochin while the evening breeze blew in from the Arabian Sea, talking about the mango trees, lemon trees, roses, jasmine and crotons we would have. "And a front verandah and a back verandah," said my mother. "Will we have a swing?" I asked. "And a swing," she said.

Kausalya had brought me up as a fully entitled modern child who would gradually grow up; not the way Indian girls had been brought up for centuries to assume heavy family responsibilities at a very early age; not the way Kanti had scratched out her survival.

We unraveled as a social unit within barely a year of my mother's death. My father began to erupt in sudden, violent rages and Kanti found that she had taken on far too much in her precarious state of health. I grew increasingly dysfunctional and my school grades plummeted. Forty years later when some of my Delhi schoolmates and I reconnected in some very pleasant reunions, my classmate Lalima told me that they had nudged each other when it was my turn to read aloud. I usually had to be called to attention by the teacher from staring absently at nothing, "eyes totally blank, uncaring of which teacher came or went," she said. "You were all there when you *were* there. But were you dead or alive that day, was the question."

My brother, sister and father became a family

within the family while Kanti and I found ourselves the outsiders. Kanti and I longed for my father's affection but could not pay the price of being the silent servitors that he expected us to be. My aunt had done an incredibly gallant thing in disrupting her own carefully constructed life to take us on and my father did not lift a finger to help or think about the effort required by a single, working lady of fifty of uncertain health to suddenly look after four people. Grand-aunt Vishali despatched cook after cook from Madras but they invariably felt lonely on the north campus of Delhi University and begged to go back, while nobody suitable seemed locally available.

Kanti gave me a number of duties around the house and insisted that my father had to "jolly well pitch in". He was told to oversee my brother's washing and dressing at least, which he did with audibly bad grace. But I never once heard my aunt say, "They're your children," to him, and her colleagues, who saw the way things were going, told me in later years that she never once complained about having to bring us up virtually single-handed those first few years until her health gave way.

My brother and sister began to adapt fairly soon while I floundered in our new existence, dreading my father's outbursts, which did not seem to need much of a trigger. Almost everything I said or did upset him and I lacked the sense or the survival instinct to realise that it was my mother who had borne me up entirely. Without her, my place in the family had dropped to the bottom; I was no longer Kausalya's cherished first-born. It was evident that my father now actively disliked me, exploding whether I stayed silent or rashly responded to something my brother and sister said.

Kanti sat frozen without a word of protest watching my father thrash me with whatever came to hand, a belt, a slipper, a stick. This was a double betrayal. My mother had whacked me sometimes when irritated but never so hard, never in such blind rage. My father was six feet tall and very strong those days from the basket-ball he was used to playing and if I turned to run, he caught me easily in Kanti's little flat. My father never laid a finger on my brother and sister but held them close. I wondered if he would have behaved differently had I been his eldest son, not his eldest daughter.

My father took to disappearing after work from his office in Shastri Bhavan to the Law Institute Library, where he sat all evening working on a doctoral dissertation. Years later, after he obtained his PhD in tax law from Bombay University, his thesis was published as a book called *Honey for Caesar: Loopholes in Tax Avoidance and Evasion*. The 'honey' came from the maxim of the ancient strategist Chanakya that a wise ruler taxed his subjects just enough; the way bees extracted nectar from flowers to make honey with. 'Caesar' meant 'the state' as in *'Render therefore unto Caesar the things which are Caesar's'* that Jesus said about paying tax. Like his mother Lalita, my father turned to study for consolation.

My father and I held on to a belief that my mother had somehow survived the air crash and was wandering about somewhere, having lost her memory. She would show up suddenly at the door and all would be well again. The irrational hope died with her first death anniversary. My father was discovered to have diabetes and since there was no more basket-ball to be had, he took to playing tennis and eating carefully.

I had been found admission halfway through term in Class Ten at Springdales School, Pusa Road. Lalita Kumaramangalam, whose father, a senior Cabinet minister, had died in the same air crash as my mother, was my classmate and sat next to me. Lalita took me home to lunch to meet her mother Kalyani, who fed us like little princesses. There was *kheer kamala* at the end, a fragrant Bengali *payasam* with oranges in it. It brought Calcutta back with a rush, memories of my mother making Bengali delicacies for me during Pujo and joining the ladies in our Poorna Das Road compound to chop vegetables for the communal feast. They had dressed me up as young Krishna for the evening cultural programme and the big girls had danced around me while I stood on a high stool with my ankles crossed, a flute held to my lips.

Our class at Springdales was taken that first winter in Delhi to the gardens of Teen Murti House, the official home of our first Prime Minister, Pundit Nehru, which had been turned into a museum and library after his death. We were taken to see the *Shankar's Weekly* inter-school painting competition being held in the Teen Murti House gardens that year. I had my first glimpse then of Nehru's daughter, Mrs Indira Gandhi, our then Prime Minister, looking chic and lovely in a green silk sari and laughing amid the beaming press of children and teachers. "I'm trying to *inch* my way forward," I heard her say. Lalita was taken to greet her and since I was standing next to Lalita, I was gently pushed forward too and bobbed my head shyly and whispered, "Good afternoon, Ma'am." She smiled very nicely at us and asked us how we liked the pictures. I was too paralyzed by shyness to say another word and Lalita answered for us.

After a while, a girl with a long plait, in a green Delhi Public School blazer, appeared at my side and asked me my name. "I'm Bindiya Loomba," she said gently. The well-known trade-unionist Satish Loomba had died in the same air crash as my mother and Lalita's father. This had to be his daughter. I put out my hand and Bindiya held it. We spoke a little and stood quietly looking at each other, and after a bit, Bindiya pressed my hand and left. I never saw her again but I never forgot her.

There was no school bus from Springdales to the north campus those days and I walked through the winter morning fog from Probyn Road, where we lived, to the bus stop at Kingsway Camp where Lord Curzon had set up a tented city for the Delhi Durbar of 1911. Great-grandfather Raghavaiyya had been made a Rao Bahadur then in faraway Chittoor. I went past many huge buffaloes setting out to graze. They would loom out of the mist and I learned to look out for them after my first scream of fright.

My mother had seen to it that I was never left alone but now I found that I had to watch out for men on the road, at the bus stop and on the bus who tried to touch me and rub against me. To try and discourage them, I took to carrying the dividers from my old Cochin compass box in my hand. My school was in west Delhi and my teachers asked a classmate, Pheroza Jhabvala, if I could get a ride back with her to north Delhi, up to where she lived on Rajpur Road in the old British area of Civil Lines, and she kindly agreed.

Getting off at Rajpur Road at around four in the afternoon, I would put my satchel on my back and walk home alone through the deserted Ridge, the stretch of the Aravalis that lay between Civil Lines and Delhi University. There was a graveled path, tarred in stretches, which wound between thick jungles of thorn trees on either side, going past Flagstaff Tower, which was a Mutiny memorial, down to a big university road. Crossing that, I would walk past the old British viceregal buildings set in a large rose garden which were now the Vice-Chancellor's and Registrar's office and so to Probyn Road.

I stopped sometimes on the Ridge to look at a

The lost paradise of Hill Grange High School in Bombay and its charismatic founder, Ms Sophie Kelly, a Baghdadi Jew. The palm hut for Sukkoth was made on that balcony.

clump of wild flowers and saw many squirrels and the occasional mongoose; and sparrows, crows, mynahs and parakeets, gradually learning to recognise babblers, hoopoes and crow-pheasants. I stepped around the broken beer bottles that littered the Flagstaff Tower patch and sometimes sang *The Happy Wanderer*, a school song from Bombay.

The idyll ended when a man crossed my path on the Ridge one day and asked me to come with him to look at '*jungli kabootar*', wild pigeons in the forest. I refused politely in halting Hindi and walked away very fast. "*Apatbandhava, Anatharakshaka*", 'Friend in Danger,

Saviour of Orphans,' I prayed to Krishna as taught by my mother and thought of the story in Sister Nivedita's *Cradle Tales of Hinduism* in which a little boy was afraid to walk alone through the woods to school and prayed to Krishna for protection as told by his mother. Sri Krishna did not appear to hold my hand but no *rakshasas* pounced the next day or the next. I quickly learned to take a bus back from Gurdwara Road near school to Maurice Nagar Chowk in Delhi University. One afternoon when walking to the bus stop from school through a shortcut, I heard rapid footsteps behind me and before I could turn around a man caught hold of me. I screamed loudly and he ran away. I walked on, trying not to cry on the road, searching in my satchel for the dividers.

It had somehow not occurred to my father and Kanti that these things could happen to a fourteen-year-old schoolgirl nor was I able to share my experiences with them. I seemed to have burnt my boats. I had a black-and white wedding photo of my parents in the old studio style in my room and I cut my father out of it one evening after a very bad beating. When he found out he took to calling me The Rakshasi. I raged at the gods but also apologised to them because my mother had loved them. Nor could I break off with them since no human being seemed that interested in my doings any more. The gods were not well thought of in university circles and I soon learned to hide my need of them.

Kanti liked to remind me of great-grandfather Narayana Sastri's ability with languages—"eighteen, including Latin and Greek, are you going to let one language defeat you?"—which was hard to hear if I came home with four out of ten in Hindi Dictation and had to account for the missing marks.

Ponni had never let up on Avvai's sayings like, "*Ukamadhu kaivideyl*" never give up enthusiasm and hope, and "*Odhuvadhu ozhiyeyl*", never stop reading or learning.

But noble resolve stubbed its toe on Hindi, which had always been a problem because the schoolbooks were dull unlike the English books. I loved the old Hindi songs that my parents played on records and enjoyed declamatory poems like *Jhansi ki Rani* but it was hard to get into the textbook language. My handwriting in both Devanagari and Roman scripts was dreadful. "*Muktavali, muktavali*, I don't see a *muktavali*," my mother and Ponni would say despairingly since I did not write like 'a row of pearls', the mark of an educated person. There was no French teacher at school in Delhi, they had a Russian one instead and I could not join midway. I missed my French classes, especially the fun of learning the songs.

The songs in Delhi were very different from anything I had learned at school in Bombay and Cochin. But for the national anthem, there was not one in common. I don't think I learned a single English song at Springdales but I entered another bandwidth of very interesting northern songs. "The return of the native," said my father for we had come back to live in the old ancestral homeland after centuries and Kanti said it was easiest to enter the spirit of a place through its songs.

My school was very Left-oriented and the children of some Eastern Bloc diplomats were sent there. We were taught to sing *Red Flag*, the rousing Italian labour anthem from 1908 based on the folksongs of Lombardy - *Avanti o popolo, alla riscossa, Bandiera rossa, Bandiera rossa*. I was added to a troupe from school that was sent to the Russian Cultural Centre on Feroze Shah Road to sing on the anniversary of the October Revolution. "*Bandiera rossa la trionferà, Evviva il comunismo e la libertà,* the Red Flag will triumph, long live communism and freedom," I sang, missing Cochin that was now sanctified forever as our last home.

One evening, I assembled Kanti and my father, brother and sister for a pre-dinner concert in the living room. Kanti knew some Japanese and had taught us *Haru ga kita*, my father had taught us *O Jemima, Look at your Uncle Jim*, *Tipperary* and other World War One songs from his cadet days in the UTC, my brother was learning new songs in the Glee Club run by Param Vir, the music teacher at St Xavier's School, and my sister could sing *Row, row, row your boat* very creditably.

It "went off well" as my father liked to say and the big surprise at the end was *Bandiera Rossa*, with my brother and sister joining in when the Red Flag was to triumph. My father and Kanti began to laugh, possibly because we were so earnest and cheerful in our assurances and waved Kanti's almost-red dishcloths so mightily.

Kanti did not sing but she asked my father for a song. He cleared his throat a bit and sang one that we liked from K.L. Saigal, *Ek raja ka beta lekar udnewala ghora*, a Hindi song about a prince and a magic flying horse. We had not heard him sing for months and begged for another but this was a mistake. My father slid automatically into another Hindi song, one of Kausalya's favourites from Pankaj Mullick, *Piya milan ko jaana* which she had told me was about an *abhisarika*, a heroine stealing out to meet her beloved in the dark. My father finished it gamely but our faces had fallen midway for the tune made us think of our mother and our concert did not end well.

My brother and sister, who had been a close part of my life under my mother's regime, were almost out of it now. They were at play with children their age in the Miranda House staff quarters compound while I struggled with my homework, hating Economics, which I had never studied before. Ironically, I lived in Kanti's house but she had no time to teach me in addition to everything else she did. Joan Robinson, whom I found on Kanti's shelves, began interestingly enough with "Consider the profile of a dolphin," but everything else was brain-deadening. I found Economics a strange subject in which it seemed you began with an assumption and then found and fit the data for it. It seemed the opposite of biology and history where things existed or had happened and you looked analytically at the whys and wherefores.

I only really met my brother and sister at dinner after which they went off to sleep, my sister with my aunt and my brother with my father. Our mornings were gone in the school rush and weekends usually boiled over in conflict with my father by Sunday evening, so I took to reading in my room as long as I could, before and after my household chores.

It was strange buying new clothes on my own. I was given money and told to take a bus to Janpath to pick up cotton tops and trousers and so I did, drinking a cold coffee at Depaul's and discovering Delhi's addictive street food. I liked going around the Cottage Industries Emporium which was the best shop in Delhi, like a living museum of beautiful textiles and handicrafts.

My aunt's flat had nice things in it long before they became popular—fine *ikat* curtains, tea things for every day from Bengal Potteries, jasper green Spode from her days in England, plates from Delhi Potteries, early Fabindia napkins.

She had a Husain woodcut of a horse and only ever had her pictures framed at a shop called Kunika Chemould, like her Ram Kumar print and a Thai *kinnara* and *kinnari* on silk.

I loved the big pouffe in tooled camel leather that she had picked up at Port Said on her way to England by sea and her low wooden bookshelves with stone and ceramic horses on top, her simple lamps and rugs and bits of japonerie—a lacquer box with cranes on the lid, ceramic bud vases. She had a dark red Kashmiri lamp painted with medieval figures playing polo, with a parchment shade. Its warm, soft light was lovely to read by and I was allowed to have it in my room.

Kanti had a garden on her roof with a peach tree and a crimson frangipani in big drums, pots of red and white Easter lilies and winter boxes of nasturtium, calendula, sweet william, red carnations, pansies and phlox. She had a half-wall of sweet peas and a tub of giant hollyhocks. Leafy ficus in big Khurja planters and pink portulaca in hanging baskets came forward in summer, and a *madhumalati* creeper and pots of jasmine and hibiscus.

I hugged Kanti hard for her home, her plants and her bookshelves, unable to put it into words. They were cultural continuities.

I practiced my Hindi on the *mali*, the *dhobi*, the maid and the shopkeepers, learning new turns of phrase every day. Kanti let me have her old transistor and my first Delhi winter was cosy, with a mug of cocoa and so to bed beneath a fat cotton quilt in a snowy white cover,

a storybook by my pillow, listening to All India Radio, to Philip Neelam introduce the English songs on the '*Forces' Requests*' hour. It was one of my duties to change the quilt covers with Kanti's maid, Chameli, and we let everything fall, laughing, when Kanti said we looked like we were putting an elephant in a diaper, "*aanaikku kovanam kattara maari*" which I translated for Chameli.

I was allowed to drag a light cane lounger to the roof on holidays, pad it with quilts and cushions and read storybooks with my back to the winter sun, oranges to hand. My brother and sister were shooed up for sunshine

My sister and I in the mid-1970s.

sometimes and we had a round or two of clapping games and finger-counting games from our Cochin days like 'Once I climbed a Chinese steeple'.

The more my aunt tried to make things nice for us, fetching us blood-red Malta oranges that I loved spooning up ice-cold, taking us to the zoo and to the fairground at Pragati Maidan, to see the pictures at the National Gallery of Modern Art or to practice our fork-and-knife manners in public on Chicken Maryland and roast lamb at family restaurants in Connaught Place, the more distant my father grew. He did not want to go anywhere anymore. Kanti took to bundling us into taxis to go see the annual Shri Ram Centre *Ram Lila* and to screenings of children's films like *Black Beauty* at Sapru House.

Carnatica was gone from my life and the occasional Tambrahms I encountered seemed like nice people but living in a world of their own. A randomly-met Tambrahm girl came home for lunch and Kanti did me proud. My guest was horrified when we served her *jimikand* cutlets. "This is meat!" she said and we said, "It's yam; we know you're vegetarian." "You mean you eat meat otherwise?" she asked. This was to remain a startled Indian question all my life. Just as I helped myself to a succulent *kabab*, someone usually said, "You're a Tambrahm and you eat meat?" It could be lonely being whiskey-*sambar* with stereotypes coming at you from all quarters. Nor could you react objectively to humbug or bad behaviour in an individual from another community without being instantly slammed for 'brahminical prejudice' although you cared a snap for brahminical attitudes and taboos. There really seemed nowhere to 'belong' if you wanted to toss your own little salad, which was not even particularly aggressive or outrageous but just your own small set of choices.

I discovered a Punjabi saying that I liked very much and thought my mother would have, too, "*Chajju da chaubara na Balkh na Bukhara*", meaning 'the comfort of Chajju's little home cannot compare with even great places like Balkh and Bukhara'. There really had been a person called Chajju in Lahore in the seventeenth century who had become a byword for being quiet and content. "Sort of like Eliza Dolittle," I thought, "*All I want is a room somewhere.*" "Room in your head and room outside," said Kanti, when I shared the thought.

Kanti's friends included interesting people like Uncle

Sarvi, who was S.K. Kathpalia, a moody, good-looking bachelor in the Foreign Service; Professor K.N. Raj and his wife Sarasa; and a young Indo-British couple, Gopal and Lyn. I remembered a rainy evening in Calcutta when Kanti had come to stay and the bell had pealed late. A man with a big smile stood at the door, wiping his glasses. It was Professor Barun De, the historian, come to see Kanti. They had been a gang of young Indian academics at Oxford, he, Kanti, Amartya Sen and Jagdish Bhagawati, and gone pub-crawling in London and to plays and films. Kanti had a lovely record of Segovia playing the classical guitar, inscribed to her "From Jagdish and Padma." I enjoyed hearing Kanti's 'London gup' as she called it.

Kanti's colleagues came home often, especially Krishna Essauloff, later Mrs Rangaiyya Bedford, who taught English literature; 'Roma Mashi' from the History Department, who was Dr Rama Mitra and had a big photograph of her close friend, the late political leader Dr Ram Manohar Lohia on her wall with a garland of sandalwood shavings on it; and of course, Uma Chakravarti, U-Chak to her students.

Kanti's friends Devaki and Lakshmi Chand Jain had two little sons, Gopal and Vasu, and invited us to visit.

Devaki Aunty had been at Oxford with Kanti. Kanti told me how they had cut up their own onions and green chillies and asked the English cook to add that to their omelettes. Devaki Aunty was from an old Tambrahm family of the former Mysore state. Her father had been the Dewan or Prime Minister and her uncle was the sociologist M.N. Srinivas. She had soirees at home, called *baithak* in Hindi and called us over one evening to watch a very young Odissi dancer. The deep note of the *pakhawaj* drum was thrilling at close quarters and I began to look for announcements of Odissi performances in the paper and tell my father, but we did not go. I missed going to watch the dance and chalked it up as one more instance of deprivation. Perhaps he was too tired to go or watching the dance without my mother was not interesting since it was her passion, not his.

Krishna Aunty's former husband, Alexander Essauloff or 'Uncle Sandrik', who seemed quite seven feet tall, still lived on campus. He charmed my fourteen-year-old heart by courteously bending to kiss my hand when we were introduced. His uncle or grandfather, I was not sure who, had been someone important in Odessa at the time of the October Revolution. The Essauloffs had fled to Paris or Rome with jewels sewn into the linings of their clothes, or so went the tale. Uncle Sandrik had fought on the Italian side in World War II and was a prisoner-of-war in Delhi when Sir Maurice Gwyer was setting up Delhi University. He asked Uncle Sandrik to teach Russian in the new School of Modern European Languages at Delhi University.

With nothing to go back to in post-war Europe, Uncle Sandrik had stayed on and soon fallen in love with and married V. Krishna, the tall, young Tambrahm lecturer in the English Department at Miranda House, the new girls' college. They had a son whom we knew of as 'Tikki', named 'Vladimir Venkateswaran Essauloff' after his Russian and Tambrahm grandfathers. He was away studying in Paris then.

Uncle Sandrik told me with a straight face that when he married Krishna Aunty he thought Indian girls were romantic figures, "fairies living on rose-petals and honey," he said. "But Kreeshna put a mountain of rice on her plate, poured yoghurt all over it, mixed it all up and ate every grain." Krishna Aunty blew smoke scornfully and arched her fine eyebrows. I practised speaking in my schoolgirl French with Uncle Sandrik when we met since I had had to leave the language behind in Cochin. I missed Carnatic music lessons but my father said I did not deserve them for being such a bad girl. Kanti found me a teacher, a Tambrahm housewife who was nowhere near my 'Radha Teacher' in Cochin and did not correct me even when I knew I was singing *apaswaram* or off-key, so my lessons were stopped. I took to practicing my scales and songs from my old music notebook and asked my father to supervise my singing. But he said he did not have the time and Kanti said I should listen to as many cassettes as I could to develop *kelvi-gnyanam*, learning through listening. My mother's store of Carnatic music cassettes was discovered suddenly in a box and I took them to my room, appropriating the cassette player whenever I could to hear the songs of N.C. Vasantakokilam, M.S. Subbulakshmi and Jon Higgins, the American who sang Carnatic music. Kanti joined me sometimes in listening and translated words that I did not understand.

Kanti's long history of illness caught up with her and her joints began to hurt when she moved. The pain made her afraid and I got used to her calling out to me several times at night to be helped up. I began to swing my arms about to build their strength. She and my father barely spoke to each other anymore. Our brief sunshine with Kanti faded with her. Kausalya and Kanti had both worked so hard to make us a proper family and it was gone, just like that.

We moved in 1976 to government housing in the

My sister and friend Sagarika by our gate in the Lutyens zone, New Delhi.

Lutyens green zone in New Delhi but after a year Kanti went back to college staff quarters on the north campus, unable to stand the long journey. My sister was sent to stay with her and hated it, begging my father to let her come back, but she was too young just then to stay with us. I wished we could have changed places.

My father continued to sit late at the Law Institute Library after office and my brother stayed out all evening playing with the boys in our neighbourhood. I would come back from college to an empty house, going to the cook's quarters at the back to call out to unlock the back door. "Coffee?" he would ask and usually make me a sandwich as well. Uncles and male cousins from Madras often made trips to Delhi and stayed with us. I knew them well from several summer holidays, from when I was first put alone on a train at fifteen to Madras with strict instructions not to get off.

I usually broke the rule at longer halts like Nagpur and Arakonam Junction to stretch my legs and buy oranges or a bunch of small, sweet bananas. It was interesting to jigget along the long length of India watching the colour of the earth change from brown to rich red. This was the cotton-growing soil of the Dakshin or Deccan, called the

Carnatic from *karu nadu*, the dark earth. Curious men and women on the train wanted personal details and I smiled vaguely at them, hiding as always behind a storybook. I was teased for my blank stare, my 'screensaver face' my brother called it decades later, snapping his fingers and saying, "Earth to Akka."

While I tuned out from fellow-passengers I was not afraid of the *napumsakar*, the eunuchs or transvestites who begged on railway platforms. Ponni and Kausalya had always spoken nicely to them and told me they were to be pitied. "*Avaakitte eppovomey aashaiya, medhuva peyshu*," 'always speak affectionately and gently to them,' they had said. My mother had written a Tamil short story about a child born with its genders mixed who given away to the eunuchs by its family. They dared not keep it, fearing what people would say; another tidy despatch of loose ends by the great Indian family. My aunt Leela in Bangalore who devoted a large chunk of her time to social work remembered that story. It was written before my mother married and my aunt had been intrigued by mother's awareness of "otherness" back in the 1950s and had looked forward to meeting her, she said.

The Grand Trunk Express took forty-two hours from

Delhi to Madras in the early 1970s and it was considered a vast improvement when the Tamil Nadu Express was introduced, which took only thirty-six hours. I enjoyed those summers in Madras and Bangalore very much, getting to know my second cousins; and the summer I spent in Burnpur with my first cousins. But I was the only girl at home in New Delhi and I protested if visiting uncles or male cousins twisted my arm or pulled at my pigtails as I went by.

Such visitors were usually sports-mad six-footers who watched Test matches on TV with my father, sprawled like lords, calling out for snacks. Our cook, Balu, had a foul temper and regularly beat his wife, Raji. She would escape into our house sometimes if I was at home and sit crying in my room for a while before going back to their quarters. I did not speak of it, not knowing what to say and to whom. I always seemed to trip over the sports shoes and tennis racquets left lying around and if I told my brother at table, like my mother had told me, to pass the vegetables to others before helping himself, my father stopped me. "Leave him alone," he said, "boys will be boys."

One day the boys found me reading a mushy old

romance by Edith M. Dell that had belonged to my mother and snatched it away. They read aloud from it in exaggerated voices, which was actually quite funny but they overdid it and I yelled at them to put my book down and leave my room. "She's the Life-President of the All-India Tap-fighters Association," drawled my father and for a while my nickname among them was '*kozha shandakaari*' or 'tap-fighter', after the poor women at the Corporation taps in Madras who queued up for water in long lines with their pots and often broke out into shrill fights.

My aunt Rajam had told me on a visit to Delhi a year after Kausalya's death that my mother had seen to every detail of our previous life, "Everything," she said, in sudden fury, "She even deposited his salary cheque for him. Your father lived like a king for seventeen years."

"It was her fault," I said, "Why did she spoil him so much, just like Lalita and Kanti did? Because he was a *boy*?"

"Hold your tongue, *adigaprasangi;* don't get into worse trouble," said my aunt sharply, looking around.

Adigaprasangi meant 'chatterbox' in the sense of 'speaking out of turn' in our antiquated dialect of

Sanskritised Tamil. I was familiar with the term and considered how best to irritate my aunt to punish her a little for speaking the truth about my father. "*Sheegrama samskshiptama shollu vishayam,*" I said. It meant, 'Tell me what you have to say quickly and briefly,' in our *sh*-heavy dialect and it annoyed the Sanskrit gold medalist. "*Ashattu makku,* silly fool," she scolded and I skipped away. It was a change from being abused almost every day by my father as "*Shanian, Peedai, Daridram,*" 'Accursed One, Affliction, Misfortune.' Translated, he belonged in mytho-comics like *Amar Chitra Katha*. When the opportunity presented itself, I told him so and he snapped back that I was a "Double Rakshasi". We were like two children without their mother. It was not a Tandalam's finest hour.

I remembered my father sweeping my mother up in his arms in Calcutta while Dean Martin sang *Make me Sway* on the record-player. She had laughed in protest, her long plait swinging. I was a five-year-old playing on the floor then, safe in their love and laughter. Our home usually had records playing in the evening, K.L. Saigal, Pankaj Mullick, M.S. Subbulakshmi, Frank Sinatra and Chuck Berry. One Holi in Calcutta, my father had come back feet first, overcome by the *bhang* in the glasses of deceptively sweet, milky *thandhai*. My mother had found it very funny and he had gone around looking sheepish for a day or two.

My father enjoyed social dancing, he knew the foxtrot, the waltz and more, picked up in his early days in Bombay before he married. He wanted to take my mother dancing to places in Park Street but she felt at a disadvantage because he was so much taller and would only dance with him at home. She did not like the taste of alcohol but every New Year's Eve, he asked her to drink a tiny glass of wine or sherry with him at the stroke of midnight.

I remembered the 1965 war. We were in Bombay and had to paste blackout paper on our windows. We were told to be ready to dive under the dining table if the air raid siren sounded. My parents laughed about that but my mother kept a basket on standby with a torch, spare cells, first aid kit, biscuits and water. The siren blared suddenly one evening and I was told to vanish at once. I remembered my doll and turned to run and fetch her and my mother caught my arm and gave me a hard whack. My father had taken me away from her and held me while I hiccupped.

I remembered the 1971 war. We were in Cochin, and had the city been evacuated, my mother, as the Collector of Customs and Central Excise for Kerala, would have stayed back in the line of duty. My father had made a joke of it and said my mother was brave enough to scare off anybody. Since stories were my best medicine he told me about Madras being the only Indian city to be attacked during World War One. The German light cruiser *Emden* had quietly entered our waters on the night of 22 September 1914, fired on oil tanks in the harbour and also destroyed a light merchant ship. The *Emden* had slipped away before the British could respond properly but the Indian Navy knew its job, said my father, and nothing would happen to Cochin, which was our biggest naval base then. In fact, the Navy put an effective maritime blockade in place along both coasts, and to the southeast, INS *Godavari* caught a small Pakistani merchant ship, the *Pasni,* on her way to Karachi, which was sent under escort to Cochin. My mother had to formally inspect it with other senior port officials; and when our aircraft-carrier INS *Vikrant* had stopped by at Cochin after the war, I was allowed to go on board with others, to look at the Sea Hawks that had strafed Cox's Bazaar and Chittagong.

We had always lived in port cities and I begged to be woken up to hear the ships in harbour sound their foghorns at midnight on New Year's Eve. I was allowed to in Cochin, the last place in which we lived together as a proper family. They woke me up just in time to hear all the ships in Cochin harbour hailing 1973 and let me taste a drop of sherry, hugging, laughing and whispering "Happy New Year, Happy New Year," not wanting to wake my sleeping brother and sister inside their mosquito nets.

I thought of being walked to sleep when I was four or five years old on my father's shoulder in Calcutta, high above the ground. I was safe on his shoulder, looking drowsily down at the floor while he sang softly in Tamil, '*Kaarmukil nira Kanna vaa, kadal alai mel thuyil oyivaa, kanimozhi peshidavey vaa*,' 'Come, cloud-hued Krishna, from your rest on the waves of the sea, come, speak sweet words to me.'

My father had been cast as Goneril when his school put on *Lear*. I found that very funny but I lacked the nous in 1973 to disarm him in the only way that may have got through, to say to him as Goneril did to her father, "...

and put away/These dispositions that of late transform you/ From what you rightly are."

My superstitious Hindu heritage made me wonder as a battered teen, "That's three tragedies in a row, Narayana Sastri, Srinivasa Sastri and S. Narayanan. Is there a curse on my father's family that kicks in, every generation?"

My no-nonsense Cidambi side that sturdily believed in a benign Providence utterly rejected the idea.

The modern common sense embodied by Kausalya, Thatha and Ponni asserted itself. This was sociological, not supernatural. My father had sustained being a Tambrahm man of the old spoilt sort, well-behaved enough outside but a nervous wreck at home if called to cope with anything outside his interests or comfort zone. It was his "bad blood" of millennia outing. And it ran in me except that the rules were different for girls.

I began to turn more and more from the Bleak House as I called it to friends whose mothers made me welcome at their table, especially to Soumya, a soft-spoken Tambrahm girl in Tenth Medical. I was in Tenth Arts and she was one of the stars at school, at the top of her class, and a swimming champion. I don't quite know how we became friends since I was a wholly average student and in a different section. Her mother, whom I took to calling 'Mina Mami' in Tamil, meaning 'Aunty Mina', had a hand in it, I suspect, encouraging Soumya to ask me over to their home on Shah Jahan Road, letting me sample the traditional Tambrahm sweets they made for Dipavali, including me in family picnics to Tughlakabad Fort where we tried to save our sandwiches from the kites and monkeys and inviting me to their annual Christmas party, "the Vadama Iyer Christmas", Mami called it.

Mina Mami.

Mami expected me to sing all the old, beloved Christmas carols and English songs of my previous life with them while she played the piano. I wondered how she knew that I knew them. There was punch, plummy Christmas cake and roast chicken. I couldn't believe it. A whiskey-*sambar* family in Delhi and, coincidentally, Vadama Iyer, like I? They seemed too modern to care for that, just like us, I thought. I wondered why they were being nice to me and resolved to flee at the first hint of pity. Glowering at their piano, I ate another piece of cake and decided to wait and see.

The history was interesting, though. It was said that there were three migrations of brahmins from the north who had gone south in ancient times; the Vadama, meaning 'the Northerners' in old Tamil, in the first wave of émigrés; the Ashta Sahasram, Sanskrit for 'the Eight Thousand' families of the second wave and the Brhatcharanam, Sanskrit for 'the Multitude' of the last wave. Of these, I was a 'Vadadesha Vadama', a 'northern Northerner'. I had once seen a Tandalam family tree that went back about eleven generations to a Subrahmanya Dikshithar. I remembered that it had classical great-great-granny names like 'Kanakavalli' which was Sanskrit for 'the Golden One'. 'Ponni' meant 'the Golden One', too, in Tamil and was also the Tamil pet name for the river Kaveri.

Soumya's family was '*Kaveri karai*' like Thatha, from the Kaveri Delta. How had that heritage in this package found me in Delhi? Mina Mami's home, like Kanti's,

Soumya on holiday with me in Europe in our twenties.

had a minimalist look with beautiful accents, nothing overstated, almost austere. But the wood was good wood with a soft polish and there were touches of Indian folk art and modern Indian art on the walls, jail *dhurrys* and jasmine in bowls.

Their homes had a distinct style, tossing elements of east and west in a light, graceful, natural fit. I did not notice it in many homes in the 1970s. It was only when I went on a school trip to see the interior of Teen Murti House and saw Pundit Nehru's personal apartments that I began calling our way of 'doing up' our homes 'the Teen Murti template'.

I was mad about ballet and modern dance and saw every film, read every book I could find but had begun to keep quiet about these things at school after someone laughed at me and called me *kala angrez*, 'black English'. Miss Mukherjee, the tiny, elderly English Language teacher at Springdales, understood, though. "My father and I could have a whole conversation in Gaelic," she told me, "It did not stop us from learning Rabindra Sangeet or going to the Kalibari."

Mina Mami had actually seen Margot Fonteyn and Rudolf Nureyev dance and I wanted to hear all about it, and about every play she had seen. I had a picture on my wall of Bakst's drawing of the costume for Nijinsky in *The Afternoon of the Faun* and found myself telling Mami about it. She spoke French and after a while, when I felt it was safe, I sang *C'est Si Bon* to her from Kanti's Yves Montand records and used words that made her laugh like '*demi-mondaine*' about the old French songstress Mistinguett.

Kausalya had taken me to watch Cho's Tamil satire *Tughlaq*. Mina Mami took me to see Ebrahim Alkazi's *Tughlaq* and other great Hindi productions of the time by the National School of Drama like *Chhote Sayyid, Bade Sayyid.*

Soumya and I in our fifties on holiday with her family at Phnom Penh.

My first concert memory of Delhi is of Mami dragging me firmly by the wrist in the dark to front seats vacated by the important guests at Mavlankar Hall, the better to hear Pundit Bhimsen Joshi. We sat up all night, some years, in the Modern School grounds on Barakhamba Road listening to Pundit Ravi Shankar play in the Shankarlal Memorial concerts. I had no defence against the music especially against the deep ragas. Soumya took to passing me a hanky since I never seemed to have one. This utter collapse of *adakkam* was deeply shameful to me but my friend knew the rules, too. She never drew attention to cracks in the façade but quietly

helped restore order. Kausalya would have loved her, I thought.

Mami had been to Cambridge and was a marvelous child educationist herself, with a very famous scientist husband. They had three daughters, like my Thatha, and Mami actually began to knit me sweaters like she did for her own girls.

While I never heard Soumya's father raise his voice, her mother gave me plenty of whacks and scoldings. She could say anything she pleased to me, there was no fooling a motherless daughter. Soumya and I began a lifelong tradition of holidaying together. We went trekking in the Himalayan hills in our teens and in our twenties, we went Eurailing and youth-hostelling around Europe and in later years on holidays with her family all over Tamil Nadu and Karnataka, to Assam and Arunachal Pradesh; to Cambodia and Indonesia. I was too broke in my forties during my newspaper days to go with them to China or Egypt but she visited me in Bangkok and so did her parents during the four years I worked there in my early fifties. Mami made two visits, which restored my *amour-propre* that my father never troubled to visit despite many entreaties and the promise to meet him at the door of the plane since I was on a diplomatic assignment. It was Soumya who always found me wherever I went in India and the world, making it her business to visit me in every place I lived in after my mother's death.

Looking back, it is curious how I was allowed to visit Soumya because her family was known and vouched for but my family took no part in it. In those violent years between fourteen and eighteen, although I never spoke of that, it now seems as though mother and daughter, who were very closely bonded, took one look, understood all kinds of things and quietly went on to attach the lone wolf to their pack.

- *Nine* -

Twenty days before Delhi University opened, India shut down with the Emergency. Kanti was on the opposite side, "this time," she said, while my father, a Congress loyalist, had no fault to find with Indira Gandhi. It was almost like a replay of the uncles at Sita Sadan being pro-British while Lalita and Kanti were for freedom, except that this time Kanti had no need to whisper.

Kanti told me to stop reading novels and take an interest in politics while my father said I would do nothing of the kind as long as he paid for my food, clothes and education. They had words and Kanti called him "a pusillanimous *paapaan*," which was an anti-brahmin Dravidian Movement term for Tambrahms, *paapaan* meaning 'seer' but in a rude way; and he called her "Don Quixote", always dashing at windmills. I was not in the line of fire this time and my brother, sister and I held hands and watched them quarrel with considerable interest as if watching a play, my sister leaning up to whisper, "What's Don Cutie?"

It struck me that between these warring factions there lay a possible middle ground. Without telling my father, I put a newspaper cover on the political leader Jayaprakash Narayan's book *Towards Revolution* which was banned by the Congress government. I took to reading it under the nose of the policewomen in plainclothes who were trying to mingle inconspicuously with the girl students at the Miranda House back gate. I had become reasonably good at reading body language, having watched and learned dance and learning to be on high alert after my mother's death, keeping my own movements subdued while covertly observing the enemy and avoiding eye contact as much as possible to escape being beaten by my father and groped by the men of Delhi. In a way, it was rather like bird-watching. Rosalind Wilson, the English teacher from England at Springdales, had told me that she was getting quite good at ducks. I noticed that I achieved a modest success at spotting disguised security personnel and began to look for some every day as a private game.

There was much muffled talk through those years

On my first job in 1980 as Editorial Assistant, with Rosalind Wilson from Springdales who became the Editor of Target, the children's magazine, and hired me while we queued for a Fassbinder film at the Goethe Institut.

in Delhi University but the dam burst only after Mrs Gandhi called for a fresh General Election. Hundreds of students marched up and down the campus chanting "*Sanjay, Indira, Bansilal, nasbandi ke teen dalal*," meaning Mrs Gandhi, her son and her minister were the agents of the shocking forced sterilisation of men during the Emergency. I went to Maurice Nagar Chowk to hear the big student rally addressed by her political opponent Atal Behari Vajpayee and Vijaya Lakshmi Pandit, Nehru's sister.

Everyone knew that aunt and niece couldn't stand each other and I felt a shiver of *schadenfreude* exactly like I felt when reading C. Rajagopalachari's English translations of the *Ramayana* and *Mahabharata*. Harrowing family sagas were as Indian as the colour of my skin and I was living through my own. I felt a great affinity suddenly with *yathum oorey, yaavarum kelir*. All towns were indeed our towns and all people were our people, though not perhaps the way the Sangam poet and my mother had meant it. Vijaya Lakshmi Pandit said of Indira Gandhi's tyranny, "*Yeh toh bachpana hai,*" 'This is childishness'; and Atal Behari Vajpayee recited his Hindi poems. I found I was jammed between a lamp post and a

Bajaj scooter with a man on it. He slid his leg against mine, shook his head in admiration of Vajpayee's verse and told me, leaning unnecessarily close, "He is a visionary poet." I fled from this encounter with democracy at work.

Like everyone else, I seemed steeped in all kinds of theatre. I auditioned with many others for Barry John's production of *Jesus Christ Superstar* in the St Stephen's College chapel, singing Mary Magdalen's song *I Don't Know How to Love Him,* and was thrilled to be given a minor place in the chorus. The rehearsals were to be held

Rosa, second from left, and I, extreme right, after 'modelling' at the Armed Forces Wives Association farewell party for the wife of Admiral Cursetji, Chief of Naval Staff, 1979. Rosa choreographed the show.

in Defence Colony in south Delhi and we were to bus it there and back from the north campus. I was to go with a kind, lovely classmate called 'Rosa', Anita Kaul, really, who was to become a staunch friend for the long haul, like Soumya. We called her 'Fresher London' in our First Year since she had been sent to Miranda House from England.

But Kanti was adamant that I could not go and spoke wildly of how she could not pay her college fees at my age; did I think life was about spending my evenings at the theatre? My father stormed into my room, swept everything on my desk to the floor and told me to get out of the house and never come back. "Dido, in the ruins of Carthage," I thought, less prone now to be "*like Niobe, all tears*". I had discovered a calm-down mechanism and stole away to Kanti's rooftop garden, armed with Chiclets, to sneak a smoke. Kanti had smoked the occasional cigarette and had a very smart matchbox and cigarette case. She stopped when she took us on but

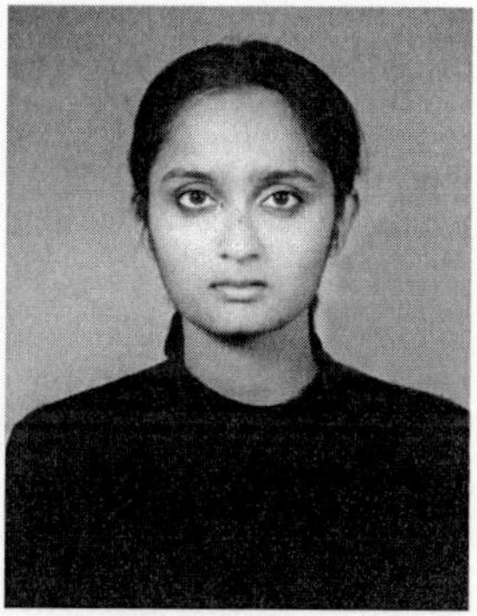

At sixteen in Miranda House.

others around us smoked. After yet another scene at home I had secretly tried a Wills Filter in defiance and found the nicotine soothing, it took the edge off my fury.

It had started in school when I had withdrawn almost wholly into storybooks, disliking every subject but English. My brother, sister and I loved to read but none of us did particularly well at school. My father was out late and my aunt was exhausted by evening so the three of us took to playing board games and dumb charades and singing and story-telling in my room, especially in the cold weather when they could not play outdoors. Without our mother to make us study, none of us were inclined to do more than our homework, which we all disliked and finished as hastily as we could to be free to play. My brother got the Junior Science Talent scholarship in his first year at St Xavier's and was the only person in its annals to lose it the next year for poor marks. My father had me trapped once and seeing his fist curled to punch me, my brother had caught his arm, got between us and taken the blow meant for me. My father had turned away for a moment and I had fled past him to my room, bolting the door. I had avoided being in the same room as him as much as I could after that and not looked at him directly for nearly a week. My sister had silently watched everything. My brother and sister realised fairly soon that their age protected them from my father's rage and began to ensure their survival by staying childish in my father's presence, coaxing and wheedling until he gave in to whatever they wanted out of him. They sounded cynical and worldly-wise by ten but their masks dropped with me. We fought, broke off, said cruel things to each other but always reached out again. However damaged we were, we could not bear to cut off ties the way my father had with his sister.

With my brother and sister at our adult-free club house

I took to plucking a hibiscus or a head of red ixora and placing it at my mother's photo as if it were an idol in the *puja* room. There was no *puja* corner in Kanti's house but shelves and shelves of plays from Aeschylus to Anouilh and Strindberg, and Jean Cocteau's *Cahiers du Cinema* and Ingmar Bergman's screenplays. She had more drama than anyone I knew, even my father.

I had two favourites among Kanti's records that we listened to sometimes between the alarums and excursions, Wanda Landowska on the harpsichord and Dinu Lipatti's last piano recital at Besançon in France; but only when we had the house to ourselves and only after Kanti promised on her honour to desist from cracks about soothing savage beasts.

After we moved when I was seventeen to the Lutyens green zone in New Delhi and Kanti had gone back to the north campus, other children in the neighbourhood took to dropping in on our adult-free club house to watch videos with us, fry up sausages, mushrooms and eggs and make stacks of cheese toast to go with the crates of 'club cola' from the Jumbo Shop at the Delhi Gymkhana Club that my sister persuaded my father to keep us steadily supplied with. We fetched Chinese food, *kababs*, éclairs and cream rolls from Khan Market and never studied if we could help it. My father locked up the video cabinet but my brother and sister found the key easily and we rented a video a day to watch when he was out of the house, using all our pocket money on food and films. I made my brother and sister watch every American musical that my mother had liked and once we discovered Damon Runyon on my father's shelves, we watched *Guys and Dolls* about six times and entertained my father with *Luck, Be a Lady Tonight* and *I've Got a Horse Right Here.*

An orange tom adopted us whom we called Mandarin followed by a black-and-white beauty of a cat that we named Cleo. Our father let us get fish scraps for the cats. They were followed by the Fab Four, a quartet of kittens, chief of whom was Palpodi, meaning 'Toothpowder' in Tamil, another marmalade tom, who thought he was a dog and ran a good way behind us on our evening walks. Hoopoes, mynahs, parakeets and jungle babblers, called *saath bhai*, meaning 'seven brothers' in Hindi were frequent flyers in our garden. For some reason 'seven brothers' was 'seven sisters' in English. We were terrified the cats would get them but they never did.

My sister and I with the cats that adopted us.

A stray had her puppies in our back garden that my brother named from the Book of Genesis because she begat so many and one day a baby vulture fell on the lawn that he fed on bread and milk and named Boogol. The wily old lizard that lived in the study was called Geronimo for his flying leaps. I had a generously-fruiting mulberry tree right outside my window and our garden was full of flowers thanks to our *mali* Kale Khan, with whom I planned the seasonals in the flower beds and the vegetable garden at the back. He suggested tubs of hydrangea near the front door once and was aghast when I burst into tears. After that he sometimes lent me his matchbox for a smoke and fetched cigarettes for me on the sly. His *inam* or douceur was a packet of Ganesh Beedi.

No aunties and uncles visited us for tea or lunch or anything and we never went anywhere unless to a classmate's house or to the home of one of our neighbourhood friends. No Tambrahms came by.

One day, however, a Tambrahm lady who was known to people that my father knew at work was to sing at a soiree at our house. This was a bolt from the blue. We had the living room cleared and spread with mats and made a place for the singer, drummer and violinist. Glasses for water and lemon *rasam* aperitif were dug out of boxes, washed and dried, trays were found for them and a south Indian caterer was called to provide *idli, vadai, upma* and *rava kesari* for a 'collation' after the concert. The violinist was an '*aruvai nayakan*', a 'prize slicer' as the Tamil term went for a string musician who sawed and scraped unmusically. The lady asked him to stop after a bit and finished her selection of songs without him. We were nervous about this bustle in our quiet lives and did not know what to say to the Tambrahm ladies, none of whom we knew and who looked about them curiously and pityingly at us. I thought of my mother and tried to offer them things to eat and drink in the proper fashion.

Except for the odd Gothic outburst, the beatings stopped after my eighteenth birthday when I fetched my purse one evening and walked out, saying I would declare myself a pauper next day to the university like Kanti had done. This worked on my father, the bureaucrat, and we even achieved an *entente cordiale* after that. I could go back peacefully to trying to be a nice girl and took to arranging flowers around the house, buying pinholders and wires and trying my hand at Ikebana, overflowing English arrangements, Indian-style garlands and flowers floating in brass bowls.

I was outraged however one day to find a tennis crotch-guard rakishly slung on the bronze Nataraja that I had seen my mother give pride of place to from our Calcutta days. "This is just not on, have some respect for my household gods," I protested and the offender, a visiting male cousin, grinned and drawled, "Keep your shirt on, *petite bourgeoise*, Shiva doesn't mind," which seemed entirely likely but a scuffle ensued into which my father walked and said, “Back off, old girl, boys will be boys.”

My father was very good about it when I went to the disco down the road at the Ambassador Hotel one evening and came back lurching. I had leaned hard on the doorbell and my father had taken me by the shoulder without a word and led me to my room with a short detour to be violently sick in. He waited for me to wash up, saw that I made it to my bed and shut the door on me.

I crawled out the next morning and found him looking strong and fit after early-morning tennis, devouring a three-egg omelette and a stack of toast lavishly buttered and spread with thick-cut marmalade. Knowing I had completely disgraced myself, I sat down and silently put my head on the table to signify that I waited for the guillotine to fall, that I expected no quarter. But all that my father said in an amused voice was, “Too much cheap liquor.” I sprang up in shock. Was that all? No medieval punishment? This extraordinary lenience created a sense of obligation in me to be careful about social drinking. My father had somehow begun to use my mother’s trick of putting me on the emotional backfoot.

He let me go out with other young people who lived in the neighbourhood, his rule being that I had to be home by eleven so that he could go to sleep in peace. My friends could stay on chatting over tea or cocoa until midnight, it was their parents' problem he said. I could go off with college friends to Simla and Manali unsupervised and when I was twenty-one, he let me have my friends over for a *dosa-kabab* party with beer and Old Monk rum on tap.

Vasupa had played the lead role, in 1977, of a professor in a brahmin village, in John Abraham's avant garde film *Agraharathil Kazhuthai* (A Donkey in a Brahmin Village) that severely satirised Tambrahm superstition and ran into a number of controversies, even being briefly banned in Tamil Nadu while the national TV channel had to cancel a telecast. However, it won the National Award for Best Feature Film in Tamil the next year, and was later rated a classic. I saw it in New Delhi at Vigyan Bhavan in the Indian panorama of the International Film Festival of India and had a spat about the film afterwards with my father who said, "It's too simple," which I countered with "And I suppose the superstitions are terribly sophisticated." "You and your aunt are well-suited," said my father and we drove home in icy mutual disdain.

However, on another visit to Delhi some years later, Vasupa, whose son Kabir had tragically fallen apart because of his drug addiction, asked me if I had smoked weed too in those teenage summer holidays and let myself be romanced by 'Kabu' whom I was very fond of and had exchanged long letters with. "I don't care if you bonked but I can't approve of drugs," he said sternly.

"No, Vasupa, it wasn't like that, how did you get that impression?" I said, not daring to look at my father. This was terrible. If my male cousins had said things about me, I didn't stand an earthly as a girl. It was disconcerting enough that second cousins to whom I was not 'forbidden' in the Tambrahm scheme of things and some of their friends, had called me "hot" and done silly things like not letting me pass by without wanting "tax" (a kiss) which I dodged and pummeled away. Being the clever fiends they were, they made up wickedly funny quizzes with lines of poetry, epigrams and literary allusions as multiple-choice answers, which they sat me down to do, sometimes holding me down at the desk by the scruff of the neck. Whichever option I picked had a double meaning and they enjoyed watching me struggle between laughter and embarrassment.

These were my personal battles and it was against the code to run tattling to their parents, who apparently asked each other things like, "Whose turn is it to have the femme fatale stay this summer?" And just as I had never told my father about the predators on the roads and buses of Delhi I had kept quiet about his first cousin who had come on a visit north and finding me alone at home, had held me close, run his hands through my long hair and revoltingly murmured that I was "a Silky Sydney". I had wriggled out of his grasp and told only my brother and sister about it. Another time, when I was away from Delhi, yet another visiting uncle had tried to fondle my sister and she had forcefully knocked him away. My brother had made sure to hover around her after that whenever he came to stay. She had been brave enough to complain to my father about this uncle but he had not believed her, she could not make him believe a word about his male cousins.

We had gone calling on Vasupa at his hotel and I felt trapped again with nowhere to run to. But a frightened peep sideways found my father looking haughtily down his nose. "I'm very sorry about Kabir's problems. But I think he was fantasising. My daughter may be a double-distilled idiot but she knows where to draw the line," he said firmly.

Vasupa nodded. "I believe her," he said, "There's been nothing like that in her letters though they were so close," and the evening carried on very civilly as if no dreadful family scandal had threatened to erupt. Vasupa even poured me a drink and told me I could smoke a cigarette with it if I wished. He laughed when I took him at his word, fished in my bag and produced a lilac Cocktail Sobranie that I fitted it into a small black holder. "Where did you get that?" said my father but forbore to investigate further. A pox on those wretched boys, I thought, and fool me for having hung out with them just because they had been nice company otherwise. There were points it seemed, to self-imposed *adakkam* as a life code. Kausalya seemed to belong to another planet. Had someone like her even existed, I asked myself in the tragic fashion of a Marie Corelli heroine. She must have, since I did, snapped my common sense and I almost chuckled aloud, for both Kanti and my father would have snorted, "Shadwell," if such maudlin thoughts had been unwisely disclosed. My brother ran away each time my father intoned from Dryden,

"Shadwell alone, of all my sons, is he
Who stands confirm'd in full stupidity.
The rest to some faint meaning make pretence,
But Shadwell never deviates into sense."

On the way home I said in a small voice, "Thank you for defending my honour, Appa." "You mean your taste," said my father. That pinched but if Kabu had gone under and his own parents couldn't help him, there was nothing I could say to my father in defence of the affectionate boy whom I knew as an amusing second cousin and fond friend, who had taken me around Madras to interesting places that nice girls normally did not go to.

While Kabir had never been north to visit us, another second cousin from Madras, big, tall, well-traveled Ashok, Raghavaiyya's eldest grandson's son, who had moved for a spell to Delhi on work, proved a fun friend. We went on butter-chicken binges to Pandara Road Market and Ashok, a keen photographer, posed me around Lodi Gardens on his days off. My brother and sister liked him, too, and we made him a member of our club house. It was all most irregular and light years away from the life led by our grannies when they had been sisters together in Sita Sadan. But were our minor 'misdeeds'—a smoke, an occasional drink, a *tandoori* chicken or a *mutton-doh-pyaza*—anything at all compared to the doings of the elder men of our family? They did not seem so to me. Thiruvalluvar, the Tamil Jain author of the ancient moral text *Tirukkural* had said, "Girls are supposed to be shy by nature. Real shyness refrains from a mean act." Ponni and Kausalya had taught me several aphorisms from the *Tirukkural* and this was their favourite.

My father forbade me to ever write to Kabir again but I wrote him a carefully cheerful letter all the same asking how he was. He did not write back. Vasupa, Zaidi Ammi and Kabu are long dead and their love and warmth seem like something from a folk tale now. I kept Kabu's clever, funny letters in a big biscuit tin that my father called my 'archives'. To my father's credit, he did not snoop in my belongings or ever ask to read my letters.

Years later, my father found a letter from Bryn Mawr College in the US tucked into one of my mother's old books. I had got ordinary scores in SAT and my father had said it was a waste of money when all I did was "mooch about and daydream". This rebuke was fully deserved for I had barely scraped into a first division. I had applied anyway for a degree in Social Anthropology to Bryn Mawr and got admission but was asked to pay for the first semester, or was it the first year, after which they said funds would be available. Perhaps they liked the way I wrote, I thought, but since I did not have brilliant grades, they wanted to see if I was really worth it. Perhaps it was their polite way of saying no.

Not knowing what to do, I had written to thank them and say that I did not have the funds. I went on to get another average score in my Master's in Linguistics from Delhi University, into which I was seduced by *Speaking of Shiva,* A.K. Ramanujan's brilliant translation of medieval Kannada poetry.

"Why did you never tell me?" said my father, about the letter from Bryn Mawr, "you know I used my Provident Fund to send your sister to America when she asked." "It didn't strike me," I said, forgetting to choose my words and my father recoiled, comfortably restored to antagonism.

"*Nishtooravalli*," he said, 'Miss Nasty'.

But he took me to the Gymkhana Club that evening

for a drink. It was all very civilised and we chatted idly about books and music as if the words and blows of years had never happened. He was amusing company with deathly malice delivered in silk. I grumbled about an older woman who was making life unbearable for me just then and my father said mildly, "She doesn't play tennis, old girl." It took a few seconds for the lethal putdown in that to register and I almost opened my eyes wide but managed to stay expressionless. My father looked blandly back. "Much better," I thought, "I couldn't endure to live permanently in an epic with tempests roaring and teapots flying."

When Kanti retired from Miranda House immobilised by her bad fall and arthritis my father had had her installed in the flat he had acquired in Madras from selling my mother's plot to a builder. But he never visited his sister. Soumya had settled in Madras by then and it was her kind, clever orthopedist husband Dr Ajit Yadav, who took charge of Kanti's medical ups and downs while Soumya made sure to visit regularly, taking her children Shreya and Akshay to see 'Kanti Paati'. Kanti liked that very much.

She had a black-and-white photograph of me atop

her TV that looked back at her in her sickbed. Friends dropped in all the time on her just like in Delhi, Uma Chakravarti dashing down to Madras from her family visits to Bangalore just to see Kanti. "She made you forget her condition," Uma said, "because she looked after you so well even from her bed. She asked you about yourself, asked after everybody, and made you talk and laugh."

When I went to Madras on my yearly catch-up, Kanti showed me her cards and letters and told me about the books she had been able to read and who had visited her and what they had said. 'Kichu Mama', the brother-in-law of a Cidambi-Tandalam cousin, lived nearby and he and his family stood staunchly by Kanti with never an awkward remark to me about my absent father.

Kanti had written a last postcard with painful effort asking me to forgive her for the torment of my teens in sad replay of Lalita's apology to her. Was there no breaking this horrible pattern? I called her to say that it was all water down the Adyar and firmly in the past. I wanted us to put it all behind and move on and be as happy and normal as possible; and not spoil the present because of the past. But their epic taint had made my father and aunt brood in separate silences when they could have cheered each other up instead.

"Kausalya would have knocked their heads together, put on a feast, given them lovely presents, asked them to sing and tell stories and everybody could have had a nice time instead of being stuck in horrid Tandalamesque tragedy," I thought, having tried and failed in my attempt to do that.

How very odd it had all been, the nature of our responses to change. Raghavaiyya, Lalita, Kanti, Thatha, Ponni and Kausalya belonged to the light. In my view, the Tandalam men, despite their advantages of birth, intelligence, good looks and self-assurance, had squandered their chances to grow; they had remained self-centred with their highly exaggerated sense of entitlement, clever but limited; and in the final analysis, feeble. As their legatee, I had been unable to imagine in my worst nightmares that I would write one day on religion, art and culture. How had that happened to someone so wholly unsuitable and with the most incidental of skills? Adrift on my own, I had been taken up by the world and given another life. Remembering the old sweetness of Janmashtami, I considered the fancy that Sri Krishna had appeared in the woods after all in the guise of those who had sustained me with their kindness and opened the door to the opportunities and experiences that had come my way. I had blessings to count and reasons to say, "Thank you for everything".

Of all people, it was that pillar of the old male establishment, the senior Shankaracharya of Kanchipuram, an ascetic monk, a *sanyasi*, who had tried to give me perspective on one of my visits to Kanchipuram, on how to live my life as a single, working woman. I had been married to a non-Tambrahm and it had ended very badly. The whiskies of Old Madras had been astonishingly non-judgemental. They had actually closed ranks around me and only said, "None of us knew them and they knew that your father did not concern himself. You took a big risk there, didn't you?"

How had they known? It was as puzzling as when Mina Mami had seemed to know without being told that I knew my Christmas carols backwards. It dawned on me then that many people in Madras had known my mother and knew Kanti, they had visited Kanti over the years and seen my photograph in her house. Madras was Kausalya's city and Kanti's city. My father's Tandalam first cousin, another Aunt Leela, who had reconnected with Kanti, asked me home to lunch. She also told me a few stories about Lalita and her sisters. To my great delight, she said they were "haughty beauties." "Were they indeed?" I murmured and, Tandalam to Tandalam, my aunt confided, "When they came to visit your grandmother in Madras, they would stand on their terrace in the evening to catch the sea breeze, you know, so pink and fair, diamonds blazing in their ears." "Goodness!" I said encouragingly, hoping for more about 'the Cidambi girls' but, disconcertingly like Kanti, my aunt had suddenly no more to say.

I got a lovely email from this aunt's brother out of the blue. He had read my burblings in the paper, he said, and told me that he had tried to meet my father in Delhi but nothing had come of it. I met a grand-daughter of Dr S. Radhakrishnan who had been to school with my father's girl cousins and to college with my mother. She knew of old scandals in my father's clan that I had never heard of from Kanti or the grand-aunts. It was mortifying that everyone knew, too, that Kanti's brother had never come to see her although she was bed-ridden. There was nowhere to duck from *itihasa*; that 'it happened that way'. People just knew. Their unspoken judgements seemed reserved for my father. He had fallen off the map of Madras; it was *mene mene tekel upharsim* with him as it had been with Srinivasa Sastri. Whom would he visit if he ever went back? He must have known it, too, for he would say, "I must go to Madras with you, I'll stay at Woodlands," but refuse to stir when I made plans.

Prema Aunty's husband had called my father all those years ago from abroad, demanding that my father "twist my arm" to marry "a known person." My witty, endearing uncle, A.P. Venkateswaran, the husband of my father's beautiful cousin Usha, had been Kausalya's classmate in Presidency College. He had tried to talk me out of that 'love marriage', "since your father has as much worldly sense as a parrot," he said bluntly, and I had hotly defended my father.

General Sundarji, who reconnected with us after years when living under high security in Delhi Cantonment, took me aside for a moment one evening in Baird Place, on a visit we made before he succumbed to illness. He had talked about music, books, theatre and travel during drinks and dinner, and said, "What will you do now? Sami doesn't seem to have a clue." I barely knew him but he had known Lalitha, Kanti and my father very well once upon a time and I had letters between my parents from 1960 that mentioned him and his first wife, Padma. Elementary *adakkam* ruled that I thanked him for the concern without bursting into tears.

A beautiful memorial evening for Sundarji was arranged after his death by his second wife, Vani, with my uncle Venkateswaran as the master of ceremonies. Space scientist Dr Raja Ramanna's piano had been brought to Baird Place for the evening and he played two of Sundarji's favourite pieces, Schubert's *Traumerai* and Beethoven's *Moonlight Sonata,* with great feeling. Afterwards (we had also listened to recordings of Hindi songs by K.L. Saigal, Carnatic music by M.S. Subbulakshmi and Frank Sinatra singing *I Did It My Way*), I had gone up to Dr Ramanna to greet him, introduce myself and thank him for the music, and found myself saying, "What a perfect whiskey-*sambar* evening it's been." Dr Ramanna had chuckled in instant understanding and said, "Have you read my English translation of the *Mukundamala*? It's in its eighteenth edition with Bharatiya Vidya Bhavan." This was a ninth century Sanskrit poem to Lord Krishna by Kulasekhara Alvar, an ancient king of the

Chera dynasty in what is now Kerala.

"Where's your father?" said my uncle Venkat.

It was embarrassing that my father had not shown up for me either when my marriage ended. People commented on it and it made me ashamed of our dysfunctional history. When I told my father about having to move to Bombay to support myself, having failed to find work in Delhi just then, he had looked up from his newspaper to say, "Oh, you'd better return my *Rajatarangini*, old girl," and gone back to reading. This was Ranjit Pandit's English translation of the 12th century Sanskrit work, the chronicles of the old Hindu kings of Kashmir and I had said, "Yes, Appa," and gone away, making sure to give it back. "It's a man's world," said Vani Sundarji, apropos of everything, though unaware of this particular exchange, and very kindly asked me to stay with her when she moved into her own flat. But I could not impose on her goodness, I had to go out and earn my living somehow.

Had 'unlucky' Lalita and Kanti felt this way, too, that they were on their own, with relatives but without family? I was thin-skinned enough to feel it when I was passed over at a Tambrahm religious ceremony by persons indirectly related to me. Some very fancy Tambrahms, whom I thought I knew rather well and were very modern, did not invite me to a wedding in the family. Were they actually afraid under the cosmopolitan veneer that I would cast a jealous, 'unlucky' eye on the happy event, I wondered. South Indians fervently believed in the evil eye, called '*kann*' in Tamil and '*nazar*' in Hindi. A woman like I, who had lapsed from the state of *sumangali* grace was thought to have the most malefic gaze of all. The centuries had willed it so. If they did not have an honourable place for me, I was not going to care, I told myself. What was the point of being Thatha's grand-daughter and Kanti's niece?

So I was wholly taken aback that the Shankaracharya, the ultimate embodiment of Hindu male orthodoxy, should take it upon himself to clinically examine my situation. "It takes society three generations to accept a radical change," he told me in Tamil. "Your mother was in the first generation of independent, working women; the spirit of the freedom movement opened the door. Your generation was hit the hardest and suffered the most as society recouped and tried to pull you back into a woman's traditional place, giving in a little but asking for much more. Things should be better for the third generation. You have *rin mukti* now, freedom from your karmic debts. Go forward and do not look back. Work hard and trust in Providence, appreciate the gifts of life."

"I find I don't relate to Carnatic music, so many words" I answered randomly, buying time to absorb his words. This had to be a crazy first, a Shankaracharya saying such things to a woman like I. I remembered that he had mysteriously vanished years ago and been discovered at the source of the holy river Kaveri where he had retreated to introspect on his role in a changing world. It was significant, I thought, that when he came back to Kanchipuram he had begun an NGO called Jan Kalyan, 'People's Welfare', and got schools, orphanages and excellent eye hospitals started. People came from all over India, especially the poor, to the eye hospitals, which were called 'Sankara Netralaya'. I knew what great-grandfather Raghavaiyya and Thatha would have felt about that shift from centuries of caste ritualism to universal public service.

I remembered calling on the Shankaracharya in Delhi at the Kamakshi temple next to Jawaharlal Nehru University and that my photographer colleague,

Mustafa, had been received just as politely as I; that the brahmin men in the Shankaracharya's entourage had cordially offered Mustafa south Indian coffee and he had been just as cordial and comfortably gone about his work photographing the interior of the temple and the Shankaracharya. A terrible crudeness was overtaking these graces across India, blurring the distinction between those were trying to effect positive change from within society and those who seemed determined to drag us back to the old, ugly ways and did not care who they hurt in the process.

The Shankaracharya looked at me inscrutably and I thought I had crossed the line and would be sent away. "It is normal to be confused in these times. If you listen to the words, really listen, your eyes will fill and overflow. Music is the only real home we have. The energy of good music is God, without it we are orphans," he said gently, sounding like my mother. I was very touched when he then tried to introduce me to some of his more well-placed adherents but got myself away. As I sped back to Madras from Kanchipuram, I accepted that I would remain culturally connected to the gods and their songs and stories. There was no plucking them out, they were part of my 'hardwiring'.

What about the tremendous attachment that I felt towards my fellow-beings, though? I understood what the Shankaracharya said about music but what mattered most to me was to have 'God' translated in everyday life as human kindness, the way Lalita, Kanti, Ponni and Kausalya seemed to have, with a world-love or soul-love that expressed itself through affectionate ways and respect. And I had found it, in my fashion.

My close friends had proved steady and loyal, making me a part of their lives. My friends were Tamil, Kashmiri, Punjabi, Haryanvi, Rajasthani, Malayali, Bengali, hardcore Hindiwala and more. Like the *modaks* that mysteriously appeared each Ganesh Chaturthi, a new sari somehow found its way to me for my birthday and for Dipavali from one or the other, as did many thoughtful presents that gave me immense pleasure because they were personal tokens of caring and affection. When I went to *puja* at the homes of my north Indian Hindu friends and the lucky red thread had to be tied on each person present, I held out my right wrist. "A woman wears it on the left wrist," corrected my friends to which I said, "I'm the *karta* (head) of my household." They nodded, and right wrist it was. Kausalya would have smiled to see it, I thought, and Kanti would have scolded, "Why do you need a thread at all?"

Just as my married women friends knit me comfortably into their lives, my gay friends were extremely kind and supportive. I had a huge trust deficit however with most hetero men and was wary and choosy about hetero male friends, dreading the cheap and easy judgements and remarks made on women even by the 'educated' ones. I had learned to find peace and dignity alone, I accepted it on good terms, and I would stay in my protective shell from that part of life. The ascetic instinct in my Tandalam blood had outed and it suited me, as it had seemed to suit great-great-grandfather Ramakrishna Sastri, great-grandfather Narayana Sastri, S. Narayanan after my mother's death, and for that matter, Kanti, except that Kanti and I also loved and needed others, their affection, and the small joys of everyday life.

Thinking over the Shankaracharya's words, I had gone, as usual, to see Rajam and Srinivasan Periappa in Madras although they had not spoken to my father in years. They helped me with all sorts of errands on my visits to see Kanti and when I thanked my uncle, he said gruffly, "Kausalya would never forgive me otherwise." Their son Sriram kept up with me as though no rift had occurred between my father and my mother's family.

I had lingered at Rajam's table, chattering away about which Kalakshetra ballet we could catch and what I should pay the reliable taxi-driver that my uncle had called to take me around next day. Glad to be able to talk about my grandparents, I gathered that Thatha and Paati

Rajam and Kausalya in their twenties.

had never missed having a son. Had it been as simple as that?

A thought about my blanked-out father had intruded then. Thatha had sold his house in Madras soon after my mother died. He had written formally to my father saying he would divide the money between his remaining daughters, Rajam and Malati, since Kausalya was gone. My father had written back at once to say that it was perfectly all right.

My father and brother knew about my trips to Madras to see Kanti and Rajam and had not said a word. When my father let the house story slip, I said, "That's all right, 'pa. The aunts didn't work and Thatha-Paati had to live with them instead of us, as planned."

"Thatha didn't like us," my brother laughed. "But you go ahead and *eeshify*. Unlike you, we three can walk into the sunset and never look back."

"*Barbary Apes Wrecking a Boudoir*," I thought crossly and saw my father, brother and sister going off hand-in-hand across the sand into a 70 mm frame, three simians into the sunset. In the foreground, coming away from them and out at the viewer was the lone gibbering monkey with grotesquely kohl-lined eyes, ribbon askew, that they had swatted aside. Fade out to the cries of two ghostly curlews flying over the lone monkey's head. I wished I could share the thought with Kanti. "*Sarasangi*," she would jeer and I would smile; part of the joke now. "I'm sure they have their versions like in *Rashomon*," I might say. Had not Kanti and I become a family within the family, too, with our own alliances? She had shared her friends with me and so had I, when I had some to share.

I wondered why Thatha had cut my father out. A Hindi saying went, '*Ghar-ghar ki kahani*,' 'That's how it is in every house', while Tolstoy had begun *Anna Karenina* with the salvo, "All happy families are alike; each unhappy family is unhappy in its own way."

What now?

Hear the other side and try asking Srinivasan Periappa why they had cut off ties with my father?

I could feel Kausalya squeezing my throat.

"I don't know and I don't want to know," I told myself, let it stay unasked and stain my neck blue.

My uncle and aunt passed away soon after and Kanti was long gone; but I kept going back to Madras to see Soumya and Mina Mami. I took to ritually looking at the sea from the rooftop of my friend's house, imagining Kausalya looking at the same sweep of the Bay of Bengal from Madras Customs House further up the shore. I could never pass the little hills outside Meenambakkam Airport without thinking, "This is the last thing on the ground that my mother saw."

Back in Delhi from one such trip, I went calling on my father with *murukku* and *thattai* from 'The Grand Sweets & Snacks', Madras.

My brother made me a nice, cold gin-and-tonic with lemons from his back-garden. "We grew up like weeds," he had said once and I looked at the mango tree, lemon tree, curryleaf tree and *madhumalati* creeper in his garden, the jasmine and frangipani. There was a dog called Pippi that his wife had rescued from the street, named for Pippi Longstocking in the children's books and a fine family of cats. One of them was a marmalade tom called 'Jinky' from 'Ajinkya', Sanskrit for 'invincible'. My brother's house was called 'Kausalya'.

My brother and I took our pre-lunch drinks to my father's room and begged him to switch off the sports channel he was watching. Things were not going well with the Indian cricket team; we had heard angry bursts of 'Billingsgate'.

My father glared at us for interrupting him and snorted when he saw the g&t. "He snorts exactly like his sister," I said and my brother chuckled. "Shake a stick at us," he invited my father, who laughed at his impudence. My father had kept up with tennis until nearly seventy-six and earned money writing opinions on tax law until he was eighty-six, appearing in court until the customary

My brother at home.

North Arcot brahmin deafness of old age began to affect him. It was Kausalya who had pushed him to get his graduate and post-graduate degrees in law. She had organised his admission, bought him his textbooks and coaxed him to study when he wanted to read a novel instead or listen to the cricket commentary on the radio or vanish to watch a Test match. "There will be plenty of time for all that. Just get through your exams first," she had said, smiling. I remembered her saying it. It had been a disciplined, orderly life for him after her death, the diabetes kept firmly under control for over forty years even if his reclusiveness had lost him the good fellowship of others. He was bedridden now at nearly eighty-nine and watched TV all day, hurling the Fifth Veda at bad umpiring, missed catches and botched shots.

I asked my father his permission to write an unexpurgated whiskey-*sambar* chronicle through the story of our little lives and he lifted a sardonic eyebrow. "I'm your first villain, am I not?" he said. "And I was a wild child, was I not?" I said carefully. He essayed an ironic salute and I suddenly saw him dashing around on the tennis court; and saying, "Sanctioned," when we wanted more pocket money or asked for chicken sandwiches from the Gymkhana Club or a Black Forest cake for our birthdays from the India International Centre. I saw him sitting with a government-approved valuer and Ganga Mami, my Tambrahm friend Jayashree's mother, as adviser, to make a fair division of my mother's modest store of jewellry into three lots, documenting it all very correctly.

My brother's son could play *An die Freude* very creditably on the keyboard thanks to his mother's strict supervision and I heard my father's voice singing it to me in Bombay. He could no longer carry a tune. It hit me that I would never hear him sing again. Why had I not taped him singing when I was the only one he had shared his books and music with? We shared my mother; we were the two who remembered a life with Kausalya in it.

I thought of the faces my father made when my mother played two favourite songs that she had on 45 rpm vinyls. She had played those rather a lot in Cochin. My sister and I listened to those songs on our separate continents and asked each other what our mother had really thought of things more than forty years ago. One was Lynn Andersen singing *I Never Promised You A Rose Garden* and the other was Nancy Sinatra singing *These*

Boots Are Gonna Walk All Over You. "She played those all the time," we told each other, giggling a bit but afraid to say more. We could not ask Kausalya, we could only listen to the words and wonder what had gone on in her head.

I looked away, struggling for *adakkam*. "Gangotri-Yamunotri," Kanti had called my eyes, for readily spouting rivers. "Mars is debilitated in her chart," an astrologer had told my friend when she insisted on asking him about my likely fate. "Cowardy custard," was our childhood term for it.

"He can't hit you now, Akka," I heard my brother say, "You write whatever you want."

"Are you writing a '*Daddy Dearest*'?" my sister had laughed over the 'phone when I asked her. "Don't hold back, Akka. I never knew our mother. I know almost nothing about our family and who did what or why. I have no stories to tell my daughter."

"It won't be easy to dredge up and I can't do a hagiography," I had said, feeling very lemming-like but privileged to have been asked to share our story, such as it was.

It amused some of our cousins that my brother and

sister still called me 'Elder Sister' in the old-fashioned, mannerly way that our mother had taught them when they learned to speak. It was yet another link with Kausalya that had proved hard to break and I had become 'Akka' to their friends, too. '*Jagat Akka*', 'elder sister to the world', teased Ashok Chauhan, my brother's best friend and my brother-by-affection, who had proved another steady, supportive friend.

My sister had taken my mother's big notebook of recipes to America; it was her most cherished possession. At her wedding in San Francisco City Hall, one of the photographs she had had taken was a re-enactment of Lalita's wedding photo with Srinivasa Sastri on a chair and Lalita standing next to him, her arm on his shoulder.

My brother and sister shared my father's keen sense of the absurd and they had my mother's marvelous hands-on skills, more than I. Instead of lemon tarts or quiche, the usual accomplishments of nice girls my age, it was Bloody Marys that my father had asked me to mix for his tennis brunch when I was eighteen. It was possibly my only household skill at that age and I said, "Not quite Varalakshmi Vratam, is it?" My father had laughed and said, "Don't let the ice run short." He told me later that

Twentyish with not many skills but can make decent Bloody Marys.

his tennis buddies had asked for my recipe to have copies made, he had been pleased with me that time.

I began to laugh, thinking of Browning's Rabbi Ben Ezra: "*What I aspired to be, and was not, comforts me.*" That was from my father, too. I thought of sitting like a little princess between him and my mother in Bombay, watching *The Man Who Knew Too Much* and Doris Day singing *Que sera, sera*.

I thought of the chances we had missed, each one of us, to draw together in our trouble. Instead we had seemed to split down the middle. Our culture was based on two terrifying epic tales of family politics, of close ties being strained to spectacular breaking point. But we could not bear to let go, our mother still murmured in us.

Aye kamale kamala-nilaye kamala-nilayah sa katham na bhavet, 'who abides in the loving-kindness of the goddess, does She not abide in them?' That was from Kausalya's daily prayer, the *Mahishasura Mardini Stotram*, an alternative world view.

I leaned into my thoughts with that. I could catch the faint snicker of men like those in Amrita Shergil's painting, lounging in temple corridors and cynically watching a band of *sumangali* women fervently prostrate to a stone *naga*, a *pipal*, a *tulsi*, a *garuda*. The mocking laughter of these men had been shared by all those other men; men on horseback, waving swords; men tilting scales in shops; men on the fields and men out at sea.

My ancestors had curtailed women's education for centuries and invented one cautionary tale after another to keep women ignorant and compliant; and these other

A photo taken for me in 2012 at the Indian Cultural Centre, Bangkok, of Buddhist nuns with a print of Amrita Shergil's Brahmins .

men had rewarded them for it and gone home to frighten their wives and daughters with these tales of nice girls and bad girls and what fasts they must keep to hang on to the roof over their heads and what badges, medals and uniforms the nice, lucky girls would get while the unlucky girls—they did not want to be unlucky girls, did they?

It was by controlling and punishing women that the men of India enforced caste said Uma Chakravarti in her academic and political writing. King Cophetua could marry the beggar maid but even if there was no likelihood of a princess marrying a woodcutter, controlling women was what many men did to maintain themselves comfortably. 'Women's rights' was not an issue separate from caste and religion. It was the very basis of caste and religion. All patriarchies enforced and sustained caste and religion by controlling women—their bodies, their reproductive rights, their personal freedoms, their cultural, and thereby social, 'acceptability'.

Uma, a Tambrahm named for the goddess like Lalita and Kanti, had fought to spell out this reality. My brother tried to spell it out too. "It's 'bros before hoes' for men, that's how the male world works," he said, wanting me to accept reality and spare myself distress. Charming, I thought. No wonder Karaikkal Ammaiyaar had pleaded with her god to turn her at once into an old woman.

Karaikkal Ammaiyaar was a sixth century saint in the old Chola country, one of the sixty-three Nayanmar. She was a young woman devotee of Shiva and received a magic mango from him one day as a mark of his favour. Her husband refused to believe it and she begged for another magic mango from her god to convince her husband that she spoke the truth. When the second magic mango appeared, her husband promptly left her to fend for herself, for she had bettered him.

The *Periya Puranam* said she had climbed Mount Kailash upside down on her head, having "given up her body" after her husband ran away. The world must have seemed upside down to her that she had been punished for being good. What an extraordinary story to tell little girls, "Be good but just good enough; you don't want to be promoted ahead of your husband, do you?"

The names on the board had gone on. Akka Mahadevi of Karnataka in the twelfth century and Lal Ded or Lalleshwari of Kashmir in the mid-fourteenth century

had become 'women saints' after they were severely ill-treated by their in-laws. They had walked away and actually wandered about naked in utter rejection of everything their societies stood for.

Going by their poetry, Akka and Lalla sounded like gentle, ardent young girls who had dreamed like any girl, of love and kindness. Akka was ten when she was married and Lalla was twelve. Lalla's mother-in-law had put a big stone on her plate and covered it with a layer of rice to make it look like a large helping and her husband had proved wholly feeble instead of growing up and taking emotional responsibility.

Tripurasundari in the south had been as cruel to Lalita and Kanti in the twentieth century as Lal Ded's mother-in-law in Kashmir in the mid-fourteenth century. Tripurasundari had not seen her 'unlucky' daughter and grand-daughter through the eyes of a woman. She had seen them through the distorted vision of the glasses put on her mind's eye by my male ancestors.

No wonder Kausalya had shielded me for as long as she could from this story world while schooling me in how to tie on a mask to deal with its reality. The *piriki* had proved a slow learner.

Meanwhile, the epic heroines were doing well and things were not easier, after all, for the third generation of Indian girls. The men had dug their heels in and the papers told us every day that it was still the wrong century for women. Baddena's transactional verse still ruled, women were still at high risk if they could not be successful service-providers, helping men be *prajavan pashuvan*, 'rich in clan and kine' like it said in the *Mantra Pushpam*, a popular chant from the *Yajur Veda*, my father's veda, which neither my father nor brother knew. It was I who enjoyed it as world poetry.

'Bhagyavantam parasuyeta ma shuram ma cha panditam,' said Kunti in the *Mahabharata*, "The lucky ones will prevail; not the valiant, nor the intelligent."

I had been neither brave nor clever but I was lucky, lucky to have prevailed against the force of five millennia in my own small fashion. *Bhagyam*, Sanskrit for 'good

The book of Shaiva saints.

fortune', did not begin to describe the enormous luck of being an educated woman in India and being able to pay for my own life, rejoicing in the love of loyal friends, grateful for the opportunities that had miraculously come my way and still on pleasant terms with Kausalya's other survivors despite the way we had gone to pieces after her death. I owed everything I had to modern India. But when the centre of our lives, a modern Indian woman,

had suddenly vanished, old India had kicked right back in and caused so much grief and harm, damaging us in ways that we still grappled with.

Nevertheless, we had shown up for our lives. The project had gone on somehow for us, and for people like us, because of the example set by those who had tried valiantly to change; innumerable Indian people like Raghavaiyya, Thatha, Lalita, Kanti and Kausalya, more valiant than we, facing far worse odds. What was going to happen to other women out there, though, the other caste; my caste?

Meanwhile there was another kind of boy growing up in India, a third generation being raised by women like Kausalya and Kanti, another kind of Indian woman.

My brother and some others in his generation were changed already thanks to their mothers, sisters, women friends and colleagues and I knew Indian fathers who absolutely cherished their daughters. I grinned, remembering a train journey to Madras from Bombay in 1970, the big, brown canvas 'hold-all' with our bedding strapped up on the top berth, our compartment arranged comfortably in two minutes by my mother. We children were being taken for a ritual head-shaving to my father's

The jamun or Java plum typical of New Delhi that we planted in 1992 for Kausalya at the Smriti Van memorial forest by the banks of the Yamuna.

ancestral deity at Tiruttani and to pay our respects to Thatha's ancestral deity at Tirupati. Our base camp in Madras was to be with Vasupa and Zaidi Ammi. Apollo Eleven had landed on the moon in July 1969 and soon after, my father had taken me by the hand to the edge of Pedder Road to watch the astronauts being driven in an open car past the cheering people of Bombay. I could swear that Neil Armstrong, the first man on the moon, had waved right at where we stood; the moon landing augured the most wonderful change on earth, ran the excited talk among the grown-ups.

As always on any journey with my mother, delicious food had appeared in vast quantities from the cane picnic basket but there were only two windows and my brother was furious about having to take turns.

"Why did you have three children?" he had raged at my mother when told to stop complaining. Kausalya had looked at him thoughtfully. "You're right, we're one too many," she had said matter-of-factly as if speaking of cheese and chutney sandwiches, "Why don't you get down at the next halt?"

My brother's jaw had dropped and he had looked around uneasily. My father had taken no notice, just the way he and Kausalya had silently endorsed Kanti's slap on my face when I was four. My sister had poked her tongue out at my brother, just a bit, not enough to catch my mother's eye. I had looked out pretending not to have heard, dying to laugh but not wanting to call attention to myself or embarrass him. It had never occurred to my brother to claim special status after that, not even after my mother's death and he was my father's sternest critic even while abiding dutifully by him.

My brother raised his glass and I drank to I knew not what.

"Bash on, regardless," I said to my fellow-travellers and father and son looked at me kindly.

- Glossary and Notes -

aeri Tamil for pond

almirah a pan-Indian term for 'cupboard' from Portuguese

appalam Tamil for fried lentil crisps, papad in Hindi and poppadom in English from Tamil pappadam, a variation of *appalam*

baai Usually spelt *bai*, a respectful Marathi term for the cleaning woman or charlady in Bombay, also the second part of women's names in North and West India such as Meerabai, Muktabai or Gangubai

Carnatic An English word for south India and 'of south India', from the Tamil *karu nadu*, the 'dark earth' or cotton-growing soil of the Indian peninsula

Dakshin 'The South' in Sanskrit, anglicised to 'the Deccan'

dal-roti a Hindi term for 'daily bread'

dargah a Sufi saint's shrine

darshan Sanskrit for 'glimpse', 'view' or 'sight of', popularly used in euphemism across India for a 'vision of God' meaning a visit to the temple with a good, satisfying experience of concentrating in prayer within sight of the focus point, the idol. Also used humorously in everyday speech as in "...and when may I have your darshan?" meaning "Long time no see" or sarcastically, to say "Get here now!" The Indian state TV channel is called Doordarshan, literally 'Far View' as in the German word for television, *Fernsehen*, literally 'Far-watching'

Dipavali Sanskrit for 'a row of lamps', meaning the Hindu Festival of Lights that occurs on a moonless night in October or November according to the Indian lunar calendar

firman a medieval sultan's decree

himsa Sanskrit for an act of violence, the opposite of *ahimsa*, non-violence

hundi pan-Indian term for the temple collection box; also a 'note of hand' with the promise to pay

idli-dosa-sambar South Indian breakfast of dumplings, crepes and vegetable stew

Kamakshi-deepam Sanskrit for 'goddess lamp', a small brass lamp with a high back etched with the image of the goddess Kamakshi, Sanskrit for 'the Love-Eyed', at the ancient temple town of Kanchipuram in Tamil Nadu, south India. Kanchipuram means 'Golden City', the origin of 'Kanchanaburi' in Thailand across the Bay of Bengal; South-East Asia was a route well-travelled by ancient seafarers from India's eastern shores all the way to China

kodai Tamil for umbrella

kooja jug, a Persian word borrowed by Tamil

kootu Tamil for a stew of vegetables and lentils

kottai-paaku Tamil for areca nuts, eaten with betel leaves as a mouth-freshener and digestive

kosmalli a salad of cucumber and *mung*

mohur pan-Indian term for a gold coin

mor-kozhambu Tamil for yoghurt soup with vegetables

mudra Sanskrit for codified hand gestures in Indian classical dance and in iconography

nagaswaram South Indian oboe, akin to the *shehnai* of the north

Nayanmar ancient Tamil saints devoted to God in the aspect of Shiva

odhuvar Tamil for ritual singer at the temple

oodhvatti incense sticks, from Persian '*oodh*' for incense, '*agarbatti*' in Hindi

paai Tamil for finely-woven grass or reed mat

pathshala Sanskrit school for Vedic priests like the Jewish yeshiva, also a modern Indian term for regular school

pachadi Tamil for a spiced yoghurt side-dish, *raita* in Hindi

paluda cold Persian pudding of thickened milk set in cones, served with fine cornflour noodles soaked in rose-syrup, sprinkled with almond and pistachio slivers; *kulfi-faluda* in Hindi

panchayat elected village council of five worthies

paneer paratha North Indian fried bread stuffed with cottage cheese

payasam milk pudding, usually made for birthdays and as ritual offering to the gods

piriki Tamil slang for 'coward'

pottu Tamil for decorative mark on the forehead for women, *bindi* in Hindi

puja Hindu prayer ceremony

raga traditional musical scales used in folk, classical, fusion and Bollywood music

Raksha Bandhan Sanskrit/Hindi for 'protection-tie', the hugely popular north Indian Hindu festival in which a sister ties a *raakhi* or yellow-and-vermilion thread as a talisman on her brother's right wrist and she in turn receives a gift from him. This ritual affirms the brother-sister bond although it comes from a husband-wife story in myth where Indra, king of the celestials, mustered the resolve to defeat a stronger enemy by looking at the 'red thread of courage' that his wife tied on his wrist before his final battle. In real times, Rani Karnavati, a 16th century Hindu queen in north India, famously sent a *raakhi* to the Mughal prince Humayun who was out on campaign, to save her kingdom from an invasion and he turned right around and marched with his army to her rescue. He was not in time to save her but he threw out the invaders and put her son on the throne, honouring the chivalrous tie conferred by the *raakhi*

rakshasi 'demoness' in Hindu mythology

rasam thin tamarind-based soup, a staple of south Indian cuisine. Its heartier version is the Anglo-Indian soup 'mulligatawny' from the Tamil for 'pepper water'

Sadhana fringe the signature hairstyle of Sadhana, a popular Bollywood film star of the 1960s

sambar thick tamarind-based south Indian soup of lentils

and vegetables eaten with steamed rice

Shaiva/Saiva literally 'of Shiva' in most Indian languages, meaning a devotee of Shiva, Shiva-worship, traditions of Shiva-worship; in Tamil Nadu, it also means 'vegetarian' as in '*Saiva saapaadu*' meaning 'vegetarian food' whereas in north India, it's '*Vaishnava*' ('of Vishnu') that signifies 'vegetarian', especially at restaurants and wayside eating places

shami kabab North Indian mincemeat patties

Shankaracharya the chosen ascetic head of one of five ancient Hindu seats of spiritual leadership, one in the Himalayas, one each on the east and west coasts of India and two in south India, which were instituted in ancient times not later than the 8th century; theories of earlier dates are under research

sondesh a traditional Bengali sweet made of milk

Sufi Muslim mystic

Suprabhatam Sanskrit for 'Good Morning', 'wake-up' prayers to the deities, sung or chanted

Talat Mahmood a leading playback singer for Hindi cinema between the 1940s and 1980s

taluk administrative unit, a sub-district

tirmanam swift, rhythmic conclusion to a dance passage in Bharata Natyam

vadai Tamil for salted, fried doughnuts or patties

vakil a pan-Indian term for 'lawyer'

Veda Sanskrit for 'Knowledge'; the first books of the Hindus that remained as oral tradition committed very exactly and consistently to memory across the Indian sub-continent, not written down until about a thousand years ago. They are considered *sruti*, Sanskrit for 'heard', meaning revealed texts that were 'heard' or 'intuited' by the ancient Hindus. There are four such texts—the Rig Veda, the Yajur Veda, the Sama Veda and the Atharva Veda. They are said to date back to between 1500 BCE and 500 BCE, to the late Bronze Age and Iron Age. Since the advent of general education in the 19th century, their content has been available in the realm of general knowledge. A full *parayanam* or complete Vedic recitation takes over seven hours. The recitation is known to heat up the body to abnormal temperatures and Vedic priests are consequently prone to stomach ulcers, to prevent which they are regularly dosed with *ghee* (clarified butter).

Venkateswara 'Lord of the Venkata Hills', a euphemism for Vishnu as the deity of the temple at Tirupati in south India *veshti-djubba* Tamil for 'sarong' and 'tunic' borrowing from Portuguese and Arabic; *dhoti-kurta* in Hindi

vetaal a very well-known ghoul in Indian folklore, bested in story by the legendary King Vikramaditya of ancient Ujjain in Central India; Ujjain was once famous, among many other reasons, as the location of the prime meridian in the old universe of discourse, just as Greenwich is today. The Arabs, those superb seafarers who took the Hindu numerals including the zero from India to the West, knew it as 'Ujaeni'. Vikramaditya, whose name means 'the Sun of Valour' in Sanskrit, is to India what King Arthur and Arthurian legends are to England. He founded a new samvat or era, the Vikram *Samvat*, which is ahead of the Gregorian calendar by fifty-seven years. The Indian calendar is still reckoned by the *Vikram Samvat*

yagnopavit Sanskrit for the 'sacred thread' worn by Hindu men, the conferring of which is an ancient rite of passage similar in purpose to its ancient cultural cousin, the Zoroastrian navjote thread ceremony, and to the Jewish bar mitzvah. A Hindu boy usually undergoes this ceremony at age eight or, as the modern practice sometimes goes, just before his wedding

zamindar pan-Indian term of Persian origin for feudal landowner

- *Acknowledgements* -

Thank you so much, Malvika Singh. But for you, I would not and could not have written this.

Many thanks, Rituraj Kapila, Sanu and Sona Kapila, for the pleasant way you've made it all happen. What a nice surprise, Rituraj and Sanu, to discover after the manuscript was in that your mother was Kanti's colleague all those years ago.

Thank you, dear Reader. Our tie is very old, too, is it not, from when two people first sat together to share a story? I've submitted this to you as one more brick in the memory wall of documenting all kinds of lives.

For the many wonderful friends along the way and for those who stayed the course, Amaladityan has it: "Those friends thou hast, and their adoption tried, Grapple them to thy soul with hoops of steel".

It took some work to gather the photographs and I have several kind people to thank.

Bangalore: Leela Sekhar, Vivek and Suchitra Sekhar, Sriram Srinivasan.

Chennai: Vidya Amarnath and Pradeep Chakravarthy for the Varalakshmi Vratam photo.

Chittoor/Hyderabad; Girija Kartikeyan.

Cochin: Commissioner Dr K.N. Raghavan and Customs House, Cochin.

Trichy: Reverend Dr. F. Andrews SJ, Principal, St Joseph's College.

Special thanks to my sister and her husband Mads Rasmussen for his help with a number of precious family photographs, especially Lalita's and Kausalya's.

This is for Thatha from a poem by Henry Austin Dobson,

Not that I think to err. I seek
To steer 'twixt blame and blindness;
I strive (as someone said in Greek)
To speak the truth with kindness.

It's a poor love that hides away, especially through confused and difficult times. So, in particular and with utmost gratitude, I praise the benign and beautiful gods, the thought of whom sustains me.